TO PADD

one love

Bless

REGGAE GOING INTERNATIONAL 1967-1976

The Bunny 'Striker' Lee Story
in his own words

as told to
Noel Hawks & Jah Floyd

PUBLISHED BY
JAMAICAN RECORDINGS PUBLISHING
Authors Noel Hawks & Jah Floyd

For information: Jamaican Recordings, PO Box 32691, London W14 0WH
First published in Great Britain in 2012 by Jamaican Recordings Publishing
Copyright Jamaican Recordings Publishing 2012
Photographs Copyright as credited
Printed in Great Britain by RAD Printing Ltd 2012
ISBN 978-0-9569991-0-8
www.jamaicanrecordings.com
℗JAMAICAN RECORDINGS 2012 ©JAMAICAN RECORDINGS 2012

Bunny Lee Then

Bunny Lee stands tall in the modern history of Jamaican music. He started in 1967 and made hits immediately. His early help came from brother in law Derrick Morgan who along with the late Slim Smith and Roy Shirley gave him the impetus to struggle in the tough Jamaican scene. Roy Shirley's 'Music Field' was his first hit and Slim gave him 'Let Me Go Girl' and The Groovers 'Do It To Me Baby'. 'Bangarang' and 'Everybody Needs Love' came a little later.

Bunny has made or been a part of Jamaica's transition from version the strictly rhythm b side of our local forty fives then dub (the bass and drum with a little rhythm popping through) that is now popular. Now his current flying cymbals are being copied by all. Bunny has led the field for many a year and possibly one man more than any other has been at his side Osbourne Ruddock or King Tubby as his fans know him.

Hits! Yes Bunny has had them including 'Wet Dream' by Max Romeo which was one of the first Jamaican records to stay on the international charts. This was on for twenty six weeks in the United Kingdom without any airplay. Yes Bunny Lee stands tall in the history of Jamaican sounds…

Liner Notes 'Bunny Lee Then' Total Sounds LP (Jamaica) circa 1976

King Street, Kingston

King Street, Kingston

CONTENTS

Introduction

"Once you hit with a sound everybody follows..." Bunny 'Striker' Lee

Omnipresent on the Jamaican musical scene for over four decades Bunny 'Striker' Lee began as an independent record promoter for Leslie Kong's Beverley's, Ken Lack's Caltone, Joe Gibbs' Amalgamated, Coxsone Dodd's Studio One and Duke Reid's Treasure Isle releases in the early Sixties. He started producing records in 1967 and his unmatched run of hits earned him the title of Jamaican Producer of the Year in 1969, 1970, 1971 & 1972. One of the first Jamaican producers to break into the UK National Charts with Max Romeo's risqué 'Wet Dream' in 1969 he was also the winner of the first Jamaican Gold Record, presented to Bunny by Tom Dowd of Atlantic Records, for 'Cherry Oh Baby' in 1971. He also holds the record for the longest consecutive period at the Number One position in the Jamaican Charts with 'Stick By Me' from John Holt in 1971. *"I have the record now for the longest selling Number One in Jamaica"*. He was instrumental in the creation of dub and released the first ever King Tubby albums. The list goes on...

Striker's standing in the Jamaican recording business is second to none for he is a man who, as well as making the hottest hits, always ensured that everyone else was looked after too. Consequently he not only commands great respect but also great affection.

"I must say Bunny Lee again! He's the one who used to motivate you. He used to boost you... because he gave me the name Prince Jammy and then King

4

Jammy. Bunny Lee gave me the name! He's always there to keep you alive... you know what I mean." Lloyd 'King Jammy' James

At one time or another Striker has been involved with every major player, and many minor players too, in the Kingston, London, New York, Miami and Toronto reggae scenes. His allegiance to his artists and musicians and an ever expanding network of friends in high and low places has meant that Striker was a man who could always get things done... and he did. Long since elevated to elder statesman status he is now a legendary figure. He is also a larger than life figure. On first hearing many of his stories can seem so far fetched as to be unbelievable and many of the moves he has made over the years truly do defy belief. Yet the facts speak for themselves and bear him out every time. There is no need for Striker to embroider his recollections for the truth is always more entertaining and *"honesty was the best policy."*

From the very beginning Striker realised the potential of releasing Jamaican music overseas; at first for expatriate Jamaicans and then for an entirely new 'crossover' audience. His original links *"in foreign"* were with Rita & Benny King's R&B Records in London and in 1968 he travelled to England for the first time to set up a deal with Island Records to release his productions. *"Island first started to put out my music on a regular basis..."* and he has never ever looked back.

"When I used to leave for England the market wasn't small like it is now... then I'd come to Canada and New York. We were just trying to get the music out to the people and most of the people who left Jamaica came to live and work in England and then Canada and America so we used to try and get the music to them." Bunny 'Striker' Lee

Always a prolific producer he licensed hundreds of recordings in London to Pama and Trojan in the late Sixties and early Seventies and still made countless records which were never released outside of Jamaica. In England Klik, Vulcan, Grounation, Count Shelly's Third World and Virgin followed, in the USA Chin Randy's, Clocktower and VP and in Canada Monica's and Micron all released a profusion of Bunny Lee productions. The man and his music were ubiquitous.

"I helped start Trojan, Pama Records with Unity then Klik Records and then Third World. I helped start off Count Shelly till Shelly became Third World. I did a lot of work with Shelly when Trojan flopped..."

Vincent's brother[1] used to release records in New York. He called himself Chin Randy's and when Vincent used to take the tunes from us he'd give them to his brother to put out ...

A man called Brad[2] in New York... he's dead now... was a very good friend of mine. Glen Adams who used to play in The Upsetters and The Wailers introduced me to him and Brad and myself did a lot of work. I first met him in New York. Brad said he was from Trench Town. He called his record store and label Clocktower after a place in Trench Town. He was from Jamaica originally... but I think Brad's mother was from Jamaica and he was born in England and went to America when he was small 'cause Brad always had that Englishman thing about him. He could talk!

He played it by ear. For instance he'd say 'You know that school where you and I went to school together? There was this woman named Miss Jones who used to teach at Trench Town School' and I'd say 'No Brad. It's Denham Town School I used to go to'. And he'd say 'Yes! It's Miss Alton at Denham Town School! You don't remember me? I was that little guy...'

He's a man who could convince you when you don't remember but he was alright! He knew everything in the business... that's how he started off his label." Bunny 'Striker' Lee

As a creator of musical trends Striker was second to none. For the best part of a decade the rest of the business hung on his every word and tried to copy his every move. On rare occasions his recordings might not have been particularly innovative but, even when he was selling other producers' ideas back to them, everyone believed it was Striker who did it first.

Although he rarely records nowadays Striker is still one of the most important people in the Jamaican music business. His rhythms and songs are endlessly recycled and sampled and he has spent the last three decades licensing, re-licensing, issuing and re-issuing his copious catalogue through a plethora of different record companies in Jamaica, England, America, Canada, Japan, France, Holland and Germany.

---

[1] Vincent: Vincent 'Randy' Chin. Born 3rd October 1937. Died 2nd February 2003. Proprietor of Randy's Record Mart and Studio 17, 17 North Parade, Kingston. Vincent was also a very accomplished record producer. Vincent's brother, Victor Chin, was the proprietor of Chin Randy's Records, 1342 St. John's Place, Brooklyn, New York, USA
[2] Brad: Glenn 'Brad' Osborne: proprietor of Brad's Records, 3756 White Plains Road, Bronx, New York, USA. Brad also released records on his Brad's & Clocktower labels

There was no route map or list of directions to follow when he first embarked on his musical journey. Many people were interested in the business and not the music but Striker is a man who knew and loved music before he ever started in the business. He has been largely responsible for the way the Jamaican music business has worked both at home and abroad and, over the years, he has been one of the few enduring constants in an ever changing cast of characters.

"And let us run with patience the race that is set before us..."
Hebrews Chapter 12 Verse 1 The Holy Bible

In October 2008 at Kingston's National Honours and Awards Ceremony Bunny 'Striker' Lee was awarded the Order of Distinction in the rank of Officer for *"more than forty years of dedicated service to the music industry"*.

Striker first asked me in the summer of 2002 *"Noel... so when are you going to write my life story?"* but I have not written Striker's life story. Instead he has told it himself, over the past six years, in an illuminating series of interviews, conversations and question and answer sessions. We hope that you enjoy reading the story of the man who has released more music than any other record producer as much as we have enjoyed putting it together.

"We have to be the tale bearers. We are still here and we thank God for that. I know there'll be some artists we've overlooked but if you want more any time you're ready we'll do it again. But if you were to write everything about me it would take forever! This is just an insight..." Bunny 'Striker' Lee

This is Bunny 'Striker' Lee's story in his own words.

Noel Hawks

Chapter 1 Early Days

Some of the people don't really know the story. Some of the people... they just really get the story... they don't know it. But I was there from the beginning. I'm around a long time. So I don't propagate any of this. I know. I know these things 'cause I was there in the midst of everything.

My name is Edward O'Sullivan Lee but my friends call me Bunny or Striker Lee. They call me Striker Lee The Hit Maker From Jamaica but plenty of people don't know where this Striker thing come from. There was a film called 'The Hitch-Hiker' with Edmond O'Brien[1] and I used to keep talking about it through it's like the first film I see. So everybody used to shorten it and say Chiker first... now some say Triker and some say Striker[2]. I started to answer to every and any... all different kind of names... until when I really come into the business and started making the hits man say *"Striker strike again"*. So the name came now and they stopped saying Triker and Chiker off of 'The Hitch-Hiker' and I made a label named Striker Lee and... you know. That's what happens in the music business.

My father was a shoemaker and my mother was a housewife. My mother, Ruby May McGaw, was from Top Mountain in St Catherine and my father was from Pear Tree Grove in St Mary... two different parishes. My father, Edward O'Connor Lee, was an elder at the St John's Presbyterian Church somewhere in

---

[1] 'The Hitch-Hiker': a 1953 film directed by Ida Lupino starring Edmond O'Brien and Frank Lovejoy who set out on a hunting trip only to be sidetracked by sadistic killer William Talman
[2] Bunny was also known as Trico Lee

Hannah Town which in those days was a good area… it's still a good area… and that's where they met. I was born on the 23rd of August, 1941 in Kingston Jubilee Hospital and I left there and went to 5 West Avenue in Greenwich Town… it was Greenwich Farm[1] then… and that's where I grew up.

There was ten of us and I'm the eldest one. Six of us survived: two girls and four boys. It was tough but we survived. My mother used to raise pigs in the back of the yard as a sideline to help my old man. When I'd come from school I used to go and pick up hog food[2]. I used to go and get yam skins from the neighbours and coconut trash and all them things to feed the pigs. We used to raise goats too… a few goats… that was school days. I went to a lady named Miss Edwards' school on East Avenue at first. What do you call them now? A prep school? There a lady named Miss Brown held my hand and taught me on the first day. I left Miss Edwards' school and went to Greenwich Town School as it was called in those days. Then to Denham Town School down near Tivoli Gardens[3] and I left Denham Town when I reached the age for Kingston Technical High School[4].

Through my parents couldn't afford it I had to start working in the days and going to the Technical School at night to study electrical engineering[5]… doing both the theory and the practical as I was studying to get my electrical licence. It's like I was going to university but in the days you did practical things and then go to evening classes and get your Diploma.

So you got to fix the outside electrical lights and all that but I fell down and damaged myself one time… in 1959… I was working on a building named West Best Bakery. The building is still standing now. I was drawing through a cable with a fish hook and wire and the wire broke and I fell and hit my back and shoulders. Luckily a scaffold broke my fall but I had a serious back injury… up to this day sometimes it still troubles me.

I was a bike mechanic after the electrician's job. I used to fix the NSU Quicklys[6] and I was a very good rider and used to do all sorts of acrobatic stuff… all type of stunts… but then I had an accident on the NSU. I started when a guy took my bike to fix it and he had it for six months. Those guys were

---

[1] Greenwich Farm, Kingston 13
[2] hog food: pig feed
[3] Denham Town Primary School, 105 North Street, Kingston 14
[4] Kingston Technical High School, 82 Hanover Street, Kingston
[5] this was in 1957
[6] NSU Quicklys: mopeds manufactured in Germany

crooks! Sometimes it's just the flywheel and they'd pull down your bike and keep it for three or four weeks and you'd just have to wait on it. When a bike came they'd send you to buy the parts as they didn't want to spend the money. Sometimes it was just the points needed adjusting or a plug wire and they'd say it needs a block and piston. They'd send you down to one of the agencies and they'd just clean up yours and sell it back to somebody else! So I used to see all the tricks they did and when I opened my bike shop everyone left them and came up to my yard. So honesty was the best policy and the people used to flock to me. We started with the NSU Quicklys and then we went over to Honda.

This was in the early Sixties when Jamaica got independence in 1962. After I gave up the bike thing I started working at Uni Motors on Spanish Town Road[1] as a desk clerk selling car parts: United Motors was a garage that used to do Vauxhall from England and Opel from Germany. I worked there for a while before I left them in 1965 and went to KIG... Kingston Industrial Garage[2]... they were the agent for Ford cars at the time. My brother Don did get me the job as a sales clerk. So I was in the motor car business and I used to be a parts salesman working the merchandise in both places.

---

[1] Uni Motors: United Motors Ltd., 427 Spanish Town Road, Kingston 11
[2] Kingston Industrial Garage: 381 Spanish Town Road, Kingston 11

Mr Martin (Old Martin), Trevor Lee, Bunny 'Striker' Lee and an NSU Quickly

BUSTER
WILD BELLS
001
HUMPTY DUMPTY
ERIC (HUMPTY DUMPTY) MORRIS
STANLEY
WITH BUSTER'S GROUP
MANUFACTURED BY WEST INDIES RECORDING CO.

KING EDWARDS
TIME
45 RPM
SHANK I SHECK
(Baba Brooks)
BABA BROOKS
DIST. BY G. EDWARDS.

BOOGIE IN MY BONES
Laurel Aitken
ISLAND RECORDS
002
R & B
RECORDS
BOX 258, KINGSTON, JAMAICA, W.I.

Hi Lite
001
PEOPLE WILL SAY WE ARE IN LOVE
Trenton Spence And His Group
163 SPANISH TOWN RD. BOX 23, JAMAICA

TROJAN
Vocals by
LORD POWER
XX02
PENNY-REEL
Played by
CALYPSO QUINTET
RECORDS LTD. JAMAICA, B.W.I.

FOR REFERENCE RECORDING ONLY
AUDIO DEVICES, Inc., NEW YORK

12

Chapter 2 Sound Systems And Record Producers

When I was growing up in the Fifties the sound systems used to play American rhythm & blues… at that time I was still going to school… 78rpm days you know, so you must know… there were a lot of sound systems in Jamaica in those days. **Real** sounds like King Edwards The Giant from my side of town. The first sound system in Jamaica was Goodies then you had a guy named Count Nick The Champ, Admiral Deans, Count Jones, Count Smith The Blues Blaster, Tom The Great Sebastian… all those sounds were before Coxsone[1] and Duke Reid[2]… Lloyd The Matador[3] and you had great sounds from Spanish Town: Ruddys[4] they were a great sound, The Wasp, Stereo, you had Mudies[5] all from Spanish Town. Lord Koos… he was a chinaman who used to own a restaurant. We used to call him Lord Koos The Universe Man. His sound was heavy! Lord Koos' deejay was a guy named Icky Man… nobody talks about him. He was with Duke Reid but he was also with Lord Koos Sound. Those guys were in the business long time and every area had their sound… in every district you have a sound. They used to play all over Jamaica you know… on

---

[1] Coxsone: Clement 'Coxsone' Dodd: Born 26th January 1932. Died 5th May 2004. Sound system controller, record shop proprietor and record producer who would later establish the Studio One recording studio

[2] Duke Reid: Arthur 'Duke' Reid Born 1915 Died 1975 sound system controller, record shop & liquor store proprietor and record producer who would later establish the Treasure Isle recording studio

[3] Lloyd The Matador: Lloyd 'Matador' Daley sound system controller, record shop proprietor and record producer

[4] Ruddys: Rudolph 'Ruddy' Redwood. Ruddys Supreme Ruler Of Sound sound system controller, club owner and record producer

[5] Mudies: Harry Mudie sound system controller, record shop proprietor and record producer

Maxfield Avenue... Nelson Road... you used to have a sound played down a Greenwich Farm at Coolie Boy's yard. The sound systems were all over Jamaica but the big guys like Coxsone and Duke Reid and Prince Buster[1] played at Forresters Hall[2]. Sound systems were like the radio station.

Mento was Jamaica's first form of music... when Coxsone first started he used to play mento before he started bringing in the rhythm & blues 78's. Coxsone used to go to America and do farm work and Duke used to go America so they brought back the American blues records so those men became kings of the arena. Duke Reid used to go abroad and bring in rhythm & blues records like Fats Waller, Lester Williams, Rosco Gordon, Smiley Lewis, Fats Domino, Louis Jordan ... Louis Jordan was like the king... and Wynonie Harris. All them cats! They were some wicked blues singers. King Edwards The Giant used to bring in some good tunes too 'cause these guys used to go abroad and do farm work and things. Duke Reid was a kind of wealthy man through he was a policeman and when they come and go with the 78's they scratched off the names and the deejays would give them their own names. If a man played a tune and they liked it he just give it a name! Tunes like 'My Baby's Gone' ... *"wake up this morning my baby is gone..."* it has a wicked tenor sax solo and we never knew the name of it! Coxsone and Duke Reid called it 'Shock Attack'[3]. When those records came out that was in the 78 days until the format change to 45 and seven inch... when they used to get a 78 cut to play on the sound we used to call it a soft wax[4]... now they call it dub.

These deejays used to lick up the place. Coxsone had Count Matchuki[5] and Duke Reid had Cuttings[6]... he's Stranger Cole's[7] brother. A man in England, we called him Shoeshine Vinny[8], him and a guy named Lou Gooden were deejays for Tom Wong... Tom The Great Sebastian. Tom's sign on tune was (sings) *"Ba da, bad ba, blue moon..."* [9] Duke Reid's sign on tune was 'My Mother's Eyes' by Tab Smith[10]... Treasure Isle Time on the radio. Those guys were great!

---

[1] Prince Buster: Cecil Bustamante 'Prince Buster' Campbell sound system controller, record shop proprietor, singer, deejay and record producer
[2] Forresters Hall, 21 North Street, Kingston
[3] 'My Baby's Gone' aka 'Shock Attack' – The Ray-O-Vacs – Decca (USA) 10" 78rpm 1951
[4] soft wax: reference disc/acetate/dub
[5] Count Matchuki: Winston 'Count Matchuki' Cooper: deejay
[6] Cuttings: Leroy 'Cuttings' Cole: deejay, selector and Duke Reid's right hand man
[7] Stranger Cole: Wilburn 'Stranger' Cole: singer
[8] Shoeshine Vinny: Duke Vin who relocated to London in 1954 to become *"the very first UK based sound system owner and operator"*
[9] 'Blue Moon' - Lynn Hope & His Tenor Sax – Aladdin (USA) 10" 78rpm 1957
[10] 'My Mother's Eyes' – Tab Smith His Fabulous Alto and Orchestra
– United (USA) 10" 78rpm 1953

They could have run Jamaica! Sir Coxsone The Down Beat came from the Down Beat 78 label and all the sound system men used to give themselves titles. Those guys used to have a whole heap of titles like Sir Coxsone Down Beat The Master of Jazz and all them things. Count Matchuki used to be Your Flash Camera Deejay. In those days you never had videos or things like that so when he appeared with the camera it was pure *"flash!"* and everybody wanted to get in the picture but it was all a gyow[1]. They never had film in the camera! If you had those pictures to look at now it would be great! Everybody wanted to get in the picture with Matchuki Your Flash Camera Deejay and people would be standing on the sidelines to see if Matchuki was coming for true. Everybody went into the dance and Matchuki would take over the mic. and start to rhyme... and when he arrived and held the mic. it was a different thing! Dance full within seconds!

Matchuki was the first rapper and gave pure nursery rhymes over the rhythm... like *"Tom the Piper get higher..."* and *"love the life you live and live the life you love 'cause love is mine to give"* and things like that. Sir Lord Comic[2] used to play King Edwards the Giant sound and his favourite words were *"Adam and Eve went up my sleeve and they never came down till Christmas Eve. Hey now! Mama is uptown shopping while father is downtown on business"*. Heh, heh, heh. That's Sir Lord Comic... he was good too. They were salesmen and they loved the business so much that Dynamics[3] employed Sir Lord Comic... I think he's passed away now. I think Matchuki's passed away too. Matchuki was the salesman for Federal[4]. Although they were rivals round the mic. they were two great friends and when Coxsone started to come up now Matchuki brought King Stitt[5].

After Matchuki left Coxsone he took over the sound from a guy named Smith... Count Smith The Blues Blaster. Smithy got sick and he gave him the sound to run and he renamed it Kingston Matchuki The Saviour. When he appeared he was dressed like Jesus in a gown with twelve men behind him. Matchuki and his twelve disciples! And a man coming before him would fan him with an old newspaper saying *"Look out... the saviour a come! Pure music!"* and there was excitement. And then a man with a handcart with some soft wax... it was probably not soft wax you know... some old records and things. And he'd send

---

[1] gyow: false/untrue
[2] Sir Lord Comic: Percy 'Sir Lord Comic' Wauchope: deejay
[3] Dynamics: 1964 to 1969 WIRL (West Indies Records Limited), 13/15 Bell Road, Kingston 11 and from 1969 Dynamic Sounds Recording Company Limited, 15 Bell Road, Kingston 11
[4] Federal Records: Federal Record Manufacturing, 220 Foreshore Road, Hagley Park PO, Kingston later Federal Record Manufacturing Company Ltd, 220 Marcus Garvey Drive, Kingston 11
[5] King Stitt: Winston 'King Stitt' Sparkes: deejay

them into a panic! They'd fan the records. *"Come out of the way! Mind you get burned! Kingston Matchuki has come now!"* These guys were some vibes men! They'd have a music[1] and they'd say: *"Anyone can name this they'll get five pounds!"* and they'd play it and a man would take up the challenge and name it. But they'd have to give the five pounds back later! You have to learn salesmanship and promotion from those old times. Those guys were great man! And they were great days…

Louis Prima became a superstar with that live album when he sang 'Robin Hood' and 'A Foggy Day In London Town'… a medley with 'Sunny Side Of The Street'. No dance couldn't keep unless they put on the Louis Prima LP[2] and Sam Butera[3]… Louis Prima's saxophonist… was a wicked horn man! You never listen to it? He came with some 45s like 'Hurry Home Baby'[4] and all those tunes were hits on the sound systems… 'Buena Sera Senorita'[5]… and a guy used to call himself Buena Sera Boop because he used to sing it on stage. You know that tune…

A sound man had to be very crafty, as you say up here, to stay on top. And that is how the record industry started in Jamaica. When the American rhythm & blues dried up Coxsone started to make his own and we used to copy the Americans when we started making our own music. Coxsone started imitating the American things… started with a boogie thing first.

After that Coxsone started calling everyone Skavoovie until he started calling everyone Jackson. He'd started calling Jack first because in every Louis Jordan tune his favourite word was Jack: *"Take me right back to the track Jack"*[6]. And Dave Bartholomew used it too so everybody was Jackson or Skavoovie and the name caught on *"Boy I go see Jackson now"* meant you were going to see Coxsone but it was Louis Jordan's pet phrase in the tune: *"Yes Jack! MacNeal, MacNeal don't steal my automobile"* [7]. Every Louis Jordan tune you listen for that name! I don't know if somebody in his band was named so but you can always hear him say it.

---

[1] a music: a record
[2] 'The Wildest Show At Tahoe' - Louis Prima - Capitol Records (USA) LP 1957
[3] Sam Butera: Born 17th August 1927. Died 3rd June 2009. Saxophonist in Louis Prima's band
[4] 'Hurry Home Baby' aka 'Five Months, Two Weeks, Two Days'
– Louis Prima -Capitol Records (USA) 7" 1956
[5] 'Buena Sera Senorita' aka 'Buona Sera' – Louis Prima - Capitol Records (USA) EP 1956
[6] 'Choo Choo Ch'Boogie' – Louis Jordan – Decca (USA) 10" 78rpm 1946
"Take me right back to the track Jack…"
[7] 'Salt Pork, West Virginia' – Louis Jordan – Decca (USA) 10" 78rpm 1946
"MacNeal, MacNeal don't steal my automobile…"

You had a lot of producers at that time because when the rhythm & blues thing started to dry up every sound man started to make his own records so there's a lot of sound men who have tunes that never came out. Baba Tewari[1] made the first rhythm & blues tune in Jamaica and one of the first producers was a man called Smith. He was a customs broker... he used to run a company shipping things to Jamaica and New York. The New York office was on White Plains Road and he had a record shop where he used to sell a lot of the American rhythm & blues records[2]. At that time I was still going to school, 78rpm days you know, so you must know! We used to clown around and listen to the latest blues at the Hi-Lite Record shop. He had an amplifier in his shop, although he was a custom broker, and in those days you had Louis Prima and all those tunes there. He made a whole heap of songs and they don't even mention him. We called him Smithy and he used to call his business Hi-Lite and he made a whole heap of hits in the early days. He never had a sound but he started to record with Keith & Enid[3] with 'Worried Over You'[4], 'Fat Man' with Derrick Morgan[5] and a couple of Owen Gray[6] hits... all those tunes are Smithy's tunes... the original 'Fat Man' was Derrick Morgan. People don't talk about Smithy now but he was a great producer... he was one of the first great record producers. Then Duke Reid started with calypso[7] and then Coxsone but Hi-Lite was the first and King Edwards followed...

And afterwards you had King Edwards The Giant come in. He was a sound system man but Hi-Lite was there before. King Edwards the Giant now he built an amplifier in about 1962 with a guy named Barry Williams. He ruled the roost! He brought down Coxsone and Duke Reid at the Lodge Hall[8] on Independence Night with an amp named Hercules Unchained... that time the Hercules films[9] did a gwaan[10]. The man a feel that amp man! He pumped down everything the sound was so heavy! The same guy, Barry Williams, built the set

---

[1] Baba Tewari: Deonarine 'Baba'/'Dada' Tewari proprietor of the Caribbean Recording Company Ltd (CRC), 118 Orange Street, Kingston and 1 Geffrard Place, off Torrington Road, Kingston. Tewari licensed records for Jamaican release from the USA and was also a record producer. His labels included Caribou, primarily for mento releases, and Downbeat which was usually used for American and Jamaican rhythm & blues recordings
[2] Simeon L Smith's Little Wonder Music Store/Hi-Lite Music Store, 163 Spanish Town Road, Kingston 13. Smithy's labels included Faith, Hero, Hi-Lite & Smiths
[3] Keith & Enid: Altamont Keith Stewart & Enid Cumberland: vocal duo
[4] 'Worried Over You' – Keith & Enid – Smiths & Hero (Jamaica)/ Blue Beat BB 006 (UK) 7" 1960
[5] 'Fat Man' – Derrick Morgan – Smith's (Jamaica) /Blue Beat BB 007 (UK) 7" 1960
[6] Owen Gray: singer
[7] 'Penny Reel' - Lord Power & The Calypso Quintet – Trojan (Jamaica) 10" 78rpm 1958
[8] Lodge Hall, Tewari Crescent, Kingston 13
[9] 'Hercules' & 'Hercules Unchained': Two Italian 'epic' films from 1959 directed by Pietro Francisci and starring Steve Reeves as Hercules
[10] did a gwaan: going on/happening

for Jack Ruby[1] and he taught Tubbys and Jammys. King Edwards The Giant was a wealthy man who used to go to America regularly. His three brothers used to live in America so they never needed a visa. They could a match any guy with money!

He started his own productions too… they just made those tunes like 'Shank I Sheck'[2] for their sound. It's an original tune but it was named after a Chinese general named Chiang Kai-shek[3] although Mrs Pottinger made one[4] but that's not the original. The original is by Baba Brooks on the King Edwards label. King Edwards had tunes with Lloyd Briscoe like *"Jonah, the master has sent me to warn you…"* [5]All those tunes belonged to King Edwards The Giant. He gave them 'nough trouble!

After that now Chris Blackwell[6] came in the business after Smithy. He came in with Wilfred 'Jackie' Edwards[7]… he's dead now… and Owen Gray and Higgs & Wilson[8] and Laurel Aitken[9]. We started to make a boogie like and how it became ska now a man called Clue J[10] said *"make the guitar go ska, ska, ska"* and the name ska was born and they strengthened the guitar sound. It's really Clue J did bring in the ska and nobody don't talk about him. A guy named Campbell[11]… he's dead now… him and Val Bennett[12] used to go *"ska, ska, ska"* right through a tune and they was a horn man and they'd solo and thing but they'd hold the ska thing right through. The ska became popular and then The Skatalites band did form with people like Jah Jerry[13]… he passed away… and Johnny Moore[14] gone too. Lester Sterling's[15] still around and him carry the Skatalites today.

---

[1] Lawrence 'Jack Ruby' Lindo: Ocho Rios based sound system operator & record producer
[2] 'Shank I Sheck' – Baba Brooks – King Edwards (Jamaica)/Rio R 61 (UK) 7" 1965
[3] Chiang Kai-shek: President of The Republic of China (Taiwan) 1948 to 1975
[4] 'Shank I Sheck' - Bobby Ellis & The Revolutionaries – High Note (Jamaica) 7" 1977
[5] 'Jonah The Master' – Lloyd Briscoe – King Edwards (Jamaica)/Island WI 187 (UK) 7" 1964
[6] Chris Blackwell: record producer and entrepreneur who moved from Kingston to London in 1962 and established Island Records
[7] Wilfred 'Jackie' Edwards: Born 1938. Died 15th August 1992. singer & song writer
[8] Higgs & Wilson: Joe Higgs. Born 3rd June 1940. Died 18th December 1999 & Roy Wilson: vocal duo
[9] Laurel Aitken: Lorenzo 'Laurel' Aitken. Born 22nd April 1927. Died 17th July 2005. singer & songwriter
[10] Clue J: Cluett 'Clue J' Johnson: double bass
[11] Campbell: Dennis 'Ska' Campbell: tenor saxophone
[12] Val Bennett: tenor saxophone
[13] Jah Jerry: Jerome 'Jah Jerry' Hines: Born 11th August 1921. Died 13th August 2007. guitar
[14] Johnny Moore: John 'Dizzy' Moore: Born 5th October 1938. Died 16th August 2008. trumpet
[15] Lester Sterling: alto saxophone

You see the ska *"checka, checka, checka"* that is the backbone of Jamaican music and it passed the beat from *"ska, ska, ska"* to *"checka, checka, checka"* and the piano a play it. If you're not doing that then it's not ska, rock steady, reggae or even the John Crow skank. Ska never stopped you know! Ska is the backbone of the music. You check it. Even in the computer music if it doesn't have the ska guitar then the piano is playing in it... so ska, whether you play it by piano or keyboard, is still the backbone of Jamaican music because after the drum and bass you have to have the ska to keep the rate. The piano's playing (sings) *"ska, ska, ska..."* You check it... then the *"checka, checka, checka"* and the organ shuffle changed it from rock steady to reggae. And then when flyers came in I get the horn man to play *"bam, bam, bam..."* sometimes with a little pattern and then take the solo like on some of Cornell's[1] tunes. Even when Jammy did the 'Sleng Teng'[2] he dubbed a ska guitar in it. So to make it Jamaican... ska never left the music. It's like an uptempo thing... through the old days it was rhythm & blues and boogie. You notice one of Laurel Aitken's first tunes *"I feel the boogie in my bones..."* [3] and gradually... right? So ska never really leave the music. Ska is always around and ska will always be around. You listen to all of the music. Everything have ska... the ska guitar or the piano playing ska. You understand?

You had some great sounds in Jamaica before even Coxsone and Duke Reid... Smith The Blues Blaster, Count Nick The Champ... Nick from the west and then came the mighty man himself Prince Buster the first Voice Of The People. He ruled the roost for a while too in the early Sixties. He had a tune called *"I told you I'd make them talk"'* or 'The Duke, The King & The Sir'[4]. The Duke is Duke Reid, The King is King Edwards and the Sir is Sir Coxsone through they all came together to try and stop the great Prince Buster but they couldn't manage it. Buster could actually sing himself and he came on so **heavy** man, believe me. So one time now Buster was running things in Jamaica. We called Buster Boop. Him and Derrick Morgan were my teachers still.

Yeah man... the great Prince Buster. Prince Buster used to work for Coxsone too and Duke Reid. Buster used to be amongst Coxsone's sound system but Buster was a man with ambition... Buster used to run sessions for Duke Reid like 'Humpty Dumpty'[5] with Eric 'Monty' Morris[1] and although he was the

---

[1] Cornell: Cornell Campbell: singer
[2] 'Under Me Sleng Teng' – Wayne Smith
– Jammy's (Jamaica) 7"/Greensleeves GRE 169 (UK) 12" 1985
[3] 'Boogie In My Bones' – Laurel Aitken – R & B (Jamaica)/Starlite ST 011 (UK) 7" 1959
[4] 'The Duke, The King & The Sir' – Prince Buster
– Prince Buster Voice Of The People (Jamaica)/Blue Beat BB 163 (UK) 7" 1963
[5] 'Humpty Dumpty' – Eric Morris – Buster Wild Bells (Jamaica)/Blue Beat BB 053 (UK) 7" 1961

producer for those tunes they were supposed to be Duke Reid's. Those tunes belonged to Duke... Derrick Morgan and them people they will tell you that. Prince Buster was an alright guy. Me and him used to spar[2]. 'Cause I used to follow most of these sound systems, like Coxsone and Duke Reid, and then I used to promote records on the radio station.

---

[1] Eric 'Monty' Morris: singer
[2] used to spar: were friends (from sparring partner)

Don Lee

22

Chapter 3 Dancing Time And Record Promotion

We used to enter a lot of jitterbug dance competitions in the days before rhythm & blues. I used to like dancing and I used to go with my friends to a thing named Teenage Dance Party[1] at JBC[2] and the programme became very popular. It was broadcast live from places like the Glass Bucket Club[3]. Sonny Bradshaw was one of the big band men and he started Teenage Dance Party and he did a lot of things for Jamaican music when he was working for the Jamaican Broadcasting Corporation. He started Teenage Dance Party... he started the Jazz Festival in Jamaica... he was the head of the Musicians Union... The Jamaican Federation Of Musicians. He brought in a lot of changes... cut down the hours musicians could play and all that. Dean Fraser and all those guys used to work for him... may his soul rest in peace.

There used to be a lot of great dancers like Castro and his brother at Teenage Dance Party. Two brothers... they're in America now. You see them on those ska films[4]. If you looked at some of them I could show you him... Castro was his last name. He was a big dancer from Teenage Dance Party. He used to tour with Carlos Malcolm[5] as a dancer... Byron Lee used to get him to dance too

---

[1] Teenage Dance Party: a record request programme on JBC, produced by jazz musician Sonny Bradshaw. Born 28th March 1926. Died 10th October 2009. At first the show only played American rhythm & blues but it began to include Jamaican records. At this time it was one of the only radio programmes, away from the sponsored shows, to feature Jamaican music

[2] JBC: Jamaica Broadcasting Corporation South Odeon Avenue, Half Way Tree, Kingston 5

[3] Glass Bucket Club: Half Way Tree Road, Kingston 5

[4] those ska films: 'This Is Ska' a 1964 documentary filmed at the Sombrero Club, Molynes Road, Kingston 10 featuring Prince Buster, Jimmy Cliff & The Maytals

[5] Carlos Malcolm: Panamanian born trumpet player and band leader Carlos Malcolm played a mixture of mento, ska and jazz. His biggest hit was 'Bonanza Ska' - Carlos Malcolm and His Afro Jamaican Rhythms – Up Beat (Jamaica)/Island WI 173 (UK) 7" 1965

because through Teenage Dance Party they were known as great dancers. We used to dance with the girls… young people would come over every Saturday and they'd tape it during the week and we'd dance. Yeah man! I was a good dancer… we had to just create some moves!

I got the plugging work through I was a popular dancer at Teenage Dance Party where they used to have a thing where they played a tune and vote if it was going to be a hit or a miss. If it was a hit it played the whole week and the people could vote to make it a hit… and say your tune was a hit it would play the whole week and catch on as it got what they now call like a power play! The hit or miss single for the whole week, you know. Me and my crew would sort out the hits to play over the weekend and from the hit or miss go on you'd get power play right through the weekend… any tune that got power play would always take on.

So I did get friendly with the different producers and if you had a record to plug you'd put it on and we'd dance to it and show the latest moves. I used to do plugging… when I say plugging I used to get their records played… for Beverley's, Coxsone and Duke Reid on Teenage Dance Party. In my lunchtime I'd take up the latest records from Duke and Coxsone from their record shops and get them played on the radio. We used to go to the different record shops and pick up records and come to Coxsone's record shop… this was when I was at Uni Motors… every lunchtime or Saturday afternoon. Saturday was when we used to close half day and I'd go to the record shops and get my little parcel of records.

I had an announcer friend who used to work on a Saturday night and we'd go to RJR[1] and JBC and call the deejays from the reception desk of the radio station and the announcer would be on. He wouldn't know we were calling from the front desk and we'd carry some girls with us and they'd say *"we're from Negril and Port Royal and Montego Bay"* and all those places! *"play that nice tune you played with that person… I can't remember the artist's name"* and they'd say *"Roy Shirley?"* so they'd say *"Yes, it sound like that…"* and not the one voice because the people would get wise so we'd have a set of girls and guys with us. It seemed like people from all over the island were requesting the record… I had the two stations locked! The tune would play ten times for the night… played all twenty times on a Saturday night. Ten times on RJR and ten times on JBC and on Monday morning every one would be in the shops asking for it… yes! So that was one way of plugging a record.

---

[1] RJR: Radio Jamaica Rediffusion, 32 Lyndhurst Road, Kingston 5

Duke and Coxsone used to be putting out something like twenty records a week. So with the ones that we liked we'd get our friends to vote on the panel to say if it's a hit or a miss. Some of them lost so it's not every one and some of them became hits by themselves! They'd just spread and a man would say *"Downbeat put out a new tune with so and so on it and it gone!"* then everyone wanted it. That's how the sound system came in too but when the radio station took up a tune and played it all ten times...

So anywhere there was a dance we'd bring records and that promoting talk and the deejay would put it on and say something about it and so we became very popular in the dancehalls. That's why we used get records from Duke Reid, Coxsone, King Edwards and all those other people and promote them. Then we'd go out on a Saturday night promoting the records. Even now with what they're hearing... if you have a man say *"this is a hit"* and although it hasn't sold one copy they'd say it sold ten thousand and everybody's going to rush out and get it.

When we used to sell records we'd go into Randy's[1] or KG's[2] or send some girls or some people to say to Miss Pat[3]: *"I want a tune named so and so. You don't have it?"* and twenty people would come in the shop and ask for the record. So when you'd mastered the record you'd say *"Miss Pat I have a record coming out y'know"* and she'd say *"Sell me five hundred of that!"* Heh, heh, heh! And KG's would say *"Bring in a thousand of it!"* Right? But it's the amount of people and 'phone calls they'd got about it and they'd probably never even heard the record! So after they'd bought them up, even if it's stupidness, they had to sell the record to make back their money and they'd push it over the counter and put it in every mail order that came in!

I also used to plug records for Ken Lack[4]. He was very good friend of mine and he was a very nice man. He was a Jamaican white man... one of the boys. Him and PJ Patterson[5] used to manage The Skatalites. He used to run an agency that brought down figurines and things from Japan and sell them into the stores in

---

[1] Randy's: Randy's Record Mart, 17 North Parade: important Kingston record shop
[2] KG's: KG's at Crossroads and KG's at Half Way Tree two important Kingston record shops
[3] Miss Pat: Vincent and Pat Chin were the proprietors of Randy's Record Mart
[4] Ken Lack: Blondel Keith Calneck. Born 1934. Died 6th June 2001. Together with PJ Patterson Ken Lack was touring and road manager for The Skatalites. He returned to his business interests dealing in hardware and household goods after the departure of Don Drummond from the band. He established the Caltone label in 1966 operating out of 15 Mark Lane, Kingston using the connections he had built up while working with The Skatalites. Surrounding himself with some of the outstanding musicians and singers of both his own and the younger generation he became *"a kind of father figure"* and mentor to his protégés. Ken Lack emigrated to the USA in the late Sixties
[5] PJ Patterson: Prime Minister of Jamaica 1992 to 2006

Jamaica... he used to sell crockery and things to the Chinese wholesalers but Ken Lack also liked music. Ken Lack always promised me a car like the one he used to drive... a white Ford Zephyr Six... and he said the car would be mine if I made 'Get On The Ball' with Roy Shirley[1] into a hit. He didn't buy me a car but gave me his own car to drive... but I couldn't even drive! Me and Phil Pratt... now me and Phil Pratt go way back from in the early Sixties... 'Sir Pratt Special'[2]. You ever hear that? Me and Phil Pratt were either side of the steering wheel. Phil let me steer the car to keep it 'pon the road and we came off the road going to Spanish Town to sell records. Heh, heh, heh... it was something else! He couldn't give me the car! I couldn't even drive it! I didn't have a licence...

Ken Lack was a nice person but just before he died he was a bitter man because it seemed that everybody had forgotten him... but we couldn't find him! He should never have left Jamaica... but some people should never leave Jamaica, you know! Ken Lack was a nice, nice man. He was one of the boys and when him done and locked up his business for the day he'd come amongst the Rasta man them... come and buy a draw for them and come amongst them and everybody loved him apart from Joe Gibbs.[3] Joe Gibbs was amongst we at those times but Joe couldn't bear Ken Lack... the other men preferred Ken Lack because Ken Lack used to socialise more. But Joe Gibbs was my friend and we'd go to the radio station and get their records played and all that. Roy Shirley[4] introduced me to Joe Gibbs and Joe asked me to plug 'Hold Them'[5] for him. He'd started with Roy Shirley and Roy brought him to me. We used to go to the radio station to promote the tune... we started out like partners but it didn't work out as Joe is a shrewd man. When the tune reached Number One he said we couldn't be partners any more ...but him alright.

I used to be a plugger for Ken Lack, Joe Gibbs, Leslie Kong, Coxsone, Duke Reid... everybody. So I was around the business but I didn't actually start for myself until 1967. While I was working at Uni Motors I used to get time off and I started moving around musicians and singers from those early days... I'd go to the studio with Derrick Morgan. He was a good teacher and I used to go to the studio and watch him recording...

---

[1] 'Get On The Ball' – Roy Shirley – Caltone (Jamaica & UK TONE 101) 7" 1967
A Number One Jamaican hit
[2] 'Sir Pratt Special' – Vin Gordon & The Supersonics
– Jon Tom (Jamaica)/Caltone TONE 103 (UK) 7" 1967
[3] Joe Gibbs: Joel 'Joe Gibbs' Gibson. Born 14th October 1942. Died 21st February 2008. Successful record shop proprietor and record producer who would later establish the Joe Gibbs recording studio
[4] Roy Shirley: Ainsworth Roy Rushton Shirley. Born 18th July 1944. Died July 2008. Highly individual, eccentric singer popularly known as 'The High Priest'
[5] 'Hold Them' – Roy Shirley - Jogibs (Jamaica)/Doctor Bird DB 1068 (UK) 7" 1967
A Number One Jamaican hit

Pluggy The Dancer and Bunny 'Striker' Lee, Toronto

BE STILL
(D. MORGAN)
DERRICK MORGAN
THE BEVERLEY ALL-STARS

THEY GOT TO COME
(PRINCE BUSTER)
Prince Buster
DRUMBAGO ORCHESTRA

ONE CUP OF COFFEE
Island Music
45 R.P.M.
WI-128
(B)
ROBERT MARLEY

LONG SHOT KICK DE BUCKET
(CROOKS, AGARD, ROBINSON)
THE PIONEERS
S.R. 072

DEAREST BEVERLEY
(J. CHAMBERS)
JIMMIE CLIFF
BEVERLEY'S ALL-STAR

THE BLAZING FIRE
(D. Morgan)
THE BEVERLEY ALL STARS

Chapter 4 Beverley's Records And Derrick Morgan... Blackhead Chinaman

Me and Derrick Morgan go back a long, long way. My first baby mother, Yvonne McLeod, was from Derrick Morgan's family... so her mother must call Derrick Morgan's mother aunt. Derrick later married my sister Nellie and became my brother in law... as a matter of fact I was in England when they got hitched... it was about 1969. Derrick and I used to move a lot... you have to say Derrick was my teacher... him and Prince Buster.

Me and Derrick started moving from he was first singing in the early Fifties with Bim & Bam... he used to imitate Little Richard[1] good, good, good![2] And

---

[1] Little Richard: Richard Wayne Penniman rhythm & blues/rock & roll singer and musician

[2] Derrick's professional debut was in Vere Johns Junior's Opportunity Hour in 1957 where he *"came first"* with his impressions of Little Richard singing 'Long Tall Sally' and 'Jenny Jenny'. Jamaica's top comedy duo Bim & Bam recruited Derrick as their singer soon after and renamed him Little Richie. Together they toured *"all the theatres in Jamaica"* and *"when Bim and Bam fell out I used to act as Bam"*

29

then he moved on and started recording with Duke Reid[1] and Coxsone and Hi-Lite, Smithy... a few others... Ruddys from Spanish Town, Count Bell The President who used to have a sound. He's passed away now. Derrick did a tune for Bell's called 'In My Heart'... *"In my heart I feel like a king..."* and those were big hits. A tune named 'Kingston 13' credited to Bell's Group[2] was on the other side. He did a lot of tunes for Prince Buster too. Derrick Morgan and Eric Monty Morris were good friends... they used to work together too. You understand?

Then comes the great Beverley's[3]... Jimmy Cliff[4] wanted Beverley's to come in the record business. The first session Jimmy Cliff did... and Beverley's first tune... was named 'Dearest Beverley'[5] and, as you know, the rest is history. 'Dearest Beverley' and Jimmy Cliff was the forerunner before anybody else. He first got Les, as we used to call Leslie Kong, interested in the music so Jimmy Cliff was a pillar and a cornerstone for Beverley's and Jimmy took Derrick to Leslie Kong.

Derrick Morgan was a singer but he also selected the artists for Beverley's. You'd come to see him and he played the piano and listened to you. If he liked your song you'd come to the studio and they'd record it. That was Derrick's job away from singing. I used to go to the studio with Derrick a lot and he used to rehearse singers like Desmond Dekker[6], George Dekker[7]... you name them.

---

[1] Derrick stayed with Bim and Bam until 1959 when *"I hear Duke Reid was taking auditions so I went to him to do some recording"*. Duke Reid did not release Derrick's songs 'Oh My' and 'Lover Boy' but kept them as exclusives and played them on acetate on his Treasure Isle Time radio show and sound system. *"He wouldn't release them until I recorded for Little Wonder. My first actual release was 'Fat Man' on their Smith's label"*. This samba based song, 'Fat Man' – Derrick Morgan – Smith's (Jamaica) /Blue Beat BB 007 (UK) 7" 1960, was a huge hit *"and after I record about six songs Duke demand me back so I started recording for him with Millicent Todd as Derrick & Patsy"*

[2] 'In My Heart' – Derrick Morgan/Kingston 13 – Bells Group
– The President (Jamaica)/Blue Beat BB 100 (UK) 7" 1962

[3] Beverley's: Record Shop & Ice Cream Parlour, 135A Orange Street, Kingston owned by Chinese Jamaican Leslie Kong. Born 1933. Died 9th August 1971. The most consistently successful record producer of the rock steady and reggae era

[4] Jimmy Cliff: James 'Jimmy Cliff' Chambers singer, songwriter and actor whose starring role in Perry Henzell's film 'The Harder They Come' in 1972 was instrumental in popularising reggae music worldwide

[5] 'Dearest Beverley' – Jimmy Cliff – Beverley's (Jamaica)/Island WI 012 (UK) 7" 1962

[6] Desmond Dekker: Desmond 'Desmond Dekker' Dacres Born 16th July 1941. Died 25th May 2006. One of Jamaica's best ever singers and songwriters and the first to have hit records on the international market. Desmond recorded exclusively for Beverley's Records until the death of Leslie Kong in 1971

[7] George Dekker: also known as George Agard and Johnny Melody a member of The Pioneers hit making vocal trio alongside Sydney Crooks & Jackie Robinson

Derrick was **the** man at Beverley's. Bob Marley was just starting out at those times and, as you know, Derrick Morgan had a very, very strong influence on Jamaican music. We call him the king of ska because when he was at Beverley's Records he discovered Bob Marley, Desmond Dekker, and even The Maytals[1]. He turned The Maytals down once and then he admitted that he'd made a mistake and they went back and worked together. Heh, heh, heh... it shows anybody can make a mistake. We still laugh about it. He said Toots sounded too much like a pocomania[2] singer!

There were four Kong brothers: Fats, Cecil, Leslie and another brother who is a Catholic priest. Leslie Kong hired a place down Greenwich Farm named Blissett House where they rehearsed. Owen Gray did some nice tunes for Beverley's too like 'Darling Patricia'[3]. Leslie Kong produced the most international hits but no-one talks about him now... Jamaican people can be funny. He's one of the founding fathers of the business... a hero of the business. He recorded Bob Marley[4] first, you know! When Derrick was on a show one time there was this youth who came on it... Robert Marley... and the people booed him off the stage and Derrick Morgan, as the man of the moment who had all the hits, said *"No! Give the youth a chance!"* And the youth sung 'Judge Not'[5] and 'One Cup Of Coffee'[6] and he brought the house down. Derrick Morgan told him to come to Beverley's and record hits. So... Derrick Morgan, Jimmy Cliff and Desmond Dekker were the backbone of Beverley's business.

Then you had Ken Boothe[7], BB Seaton and The Gaylads[8] and when The Wailers album came out on Beverley's they called it 'Best Of The Wailers'[9]. The Melodians: 'Rivers Of Babylon'[10], 'Sweet Sensation'[11], The Pioneers: 'Long Shot Kick De/The Bucket'[12]... You name them! Two big hits from Desmond

---

[1] The Maytals: one of Jamaica's most successful vocal trios, Frederick 'Toots' Hibbert, Henry 'Raleigh' Gordon & Nathaniel 'Jerry' McCarthy, also known as The Flames and The Vikings
[2] pocomania: a mixture of Christian revivalism and ancestral spirit possession
[3] 'Darling Patricia' – Owen Gray – Beverley's (Jamaica)/Island WI 002 (UK) 7" 1962
[4] Bob Marley: Born 6th February 1945. Died 11th May 1981. Before the formation of the original Wailers Robert 'Bob' Marley recorded two solo singles for Leslie Kong's Beverley's label
[5] 'Judge Not' – Robert Marley – Beverley's (Jamaica)/Island WI 088 (UK) 7" 1963
[6] 'One Cup Of Coffee' –Bobby Martell/ Robert Marley
– Beverley's (Jamaica)/Island WI 128 (UK) 7" 1963
[7] Ken Boothe: singer
[8] BB Seaton and The Gaylads: a matchless vocal trio consisting of Harris 'BB' Seaton, Winston Delano Stewart & Maurice Roberts
[9] 'The Best Of' - The Wailers – Beverley's BLP 011 (Jamaica) LP 1970
[10] 'Rivers Of Babylon' - The Melodians – Beverley's (Jamaica)/Trojan TR 9037 (UK) 7" 1970
[11] 'Sweet Sensation' – The Melodians – Beverley's (Jamaica)/Trojan TR 695 (UK) 7" 1969
[12] 'Long Shot Kick De/The Bucket' – The Pioneers
– Beverley's (Jamaica) /Trojan TR 672 (UK) 7" 1969

Dekker in the early days: '007'[1] and '(Poor Me) Israelites'[2]. You can say Derrick produced those songs because he **was** the producer... him and Leslie Kong made those tunes but Leslie Kong was the man who sat in the control room and if he didn't like it he'd say so! Leslie Kong made some great music... he was in it from ska days... a whole heap of Roland Alphonso[3] too. Some of the best tunes out on the road are Leslie Kong's but he died very early.

I remember I was looking for a tune to do (sings) *"Swing low sweet chariot coming for to carry me home..."* but I couldn't find the one I wanted... the jazz one... I think it was Dizzy Gillespie who did it and called it 'Swing Low Sweet Cadillac'[4] but I couldn't find it and then when Leslie Kong did the tune *"I looked over Jordan what do I see? A band of angels coming for to carry me home"* and I was so glad I didn't do the tune... I had a dream, you know, certain tunes you mustn't do. Then it's coming like the next week I was going to Dynamics and the news come that Leslie Kong died of a heart attack that morning. You understand?

I must tell you this. Plenty of people don't talk about him now but Leslie Kong made the most international hits before Bob Marley... '007' and '(Poor Me) Israelites' from Desmond Dekker was some of the first then 'Long Shot Kick De/The Bucket' from The Pioneers... the hit list goes on. He was there from in the ska era and he made the most chart music in the Sixties and Seventies but the younger people don't really know about Beverley's. His music was good... it speaks for itself now... and it's still in demand. 'Blazing Fire' from Derrick Morgan[5], 'Darling Patricia' from Owen Gray[6] all of those big hits from long time coming right down were on Beverley's. You know Beverley's made the most international hit tunes up to this day? I don't why he doesn't get the credit for it. I have plenty of tunes on tape from him 'cause remember I used to plug records for him. He died early and his brother Cecil used to carry it on but he wasn't really interested. Les had a son too but he wasn't interested either. Warwick Lyn[7] was working with him but after Les died he started to work with Dynamic Sounds.

---

[1] '007' – Desmond Dekker & The Aces – Beverley's (Jamaica)/Pyramid PYR 6004 (UK) 7" 1967
[2] 'Poor Me Israelites'/'Israelites' – Desmond Dekker & The Aces
- Beverley's (Jamaica)/Pyramid PYR 6058 (UK) 7" 1968 A Number One UK hit
[3] Roland Alphonso: Born 12th January 1931. Died 20th November 1998. Tenor saxophone and influential musical arranger. A founding member of The Skatalites Roland Alphonso was awarded the Order of Distinction by The Jamaican Government in 1977
[4] 'Swing Low, Sweet Cadillac' – Dizzy Gillespie – Impulse (USA) LP 1967
[5] 'The Blazing Fire' - Derrick Morgan – Beverley's (Jamaica)/Island WI 051 (UK) 7" 1963
[6] 'Darling Patricia' - Owen Gray – Beverley's (Jamaica)/Island WI 002 (UK) 1962
[7] Warwick Lyn: Born 1946. Died 10th May 2009. Recording engineer and record producer

Derrick Morgan and Prince Buster had that confrontation on record when Buster did a tune 'They Got To Come'[1] and then Derrick did one named 'Forward March'[2] for Beverley's. Well the solo in 'Forward March' was near but if you listen properly it's two different solos. Prince Buster was vexed and he said Derrick had stolen his solo and used it for the Beverley's tune[3]. Leslie Kong was Chinese and Buster sang:

"You done stole my belongings and give to your chiney man
God in heaven knows, he knows, that you are wrong
Are you a china man?
Are you a black man?
It don't need no eye glasses to see that your skin is black..."
Prince Buster: 'Black Head Chinaman'[4]

And then Derrick answered with 'The Blazing Fire' which he introduced in the Chinese language and then sung *"Be still and know I'm your superior"* so they had quite a carrying on but that rivalry thing helped to sell records too for quite a while!

Derrick Morgan still has it. Every show he goes on he steals it! Yes! One time when he was in America they used Derrick to open a show for Black Uhuru[5] and when Derrick was done everybody came out of the place! Any time Derrick goes anywhere they always like Derrick! But they have to sing before Derrick Morgan...

---

[1] 'They Got To Come' – Prince Buster
– Prince Buster Voice Of The People (Jamaica)/Dice CC 06 (UK) 7" 1962
[2] 'Forward March' – Derrick Morgan – Beverley's (Jamaica)/Island WI 011 (UK) 7" 1962
[3] *"Then I met Prince Buster and we get together and I started to record for Buster. Prince Buster and I were good friends until I left him for Beverley's and after 'Forward March' in 1962 he write a song about me called 'Black Head Chinaman'"*. Derrick explained that the *"belongings"* that Buster accused Derrick of taking from him were actually the horn players Felix 'Deadly' Hedley Bennett and Lester Sterling who had blown the solos with Derrick in 'Forward March'... *"that's what caused the disruption"*
[4] 'Black Head Chinaman' - Prince Buster - Prince Buster (Jamaica)/Dice CC 11 (UK) 7" 1963
[5] Black Uhuru: internationally successful vocal trio, Michael Rose, Derrick 'Ducky' Simpson and Sandra 'Puma' Jones, signed to Island Records in 1980

Bunny 'Striker' Lee

Leslie Kong

Bunny 'Striker' Lee

Bunny 'Striker' Lee and Prince Buster

POOR ME ISRAELITES
(D. DEKKER)
DESMOND DEKKER and THE ACES.

"UNITY"
(D. DEKKER)
DESMOND DEKKER and THE ACES.

FESTIVAL SONG 1967
BABA BOOM
THE JAMAICANS
With Tommy McCook &
The Supersonics

EVERY NIGHT
JOE WHITE
JOE WHITE & CHUCK
BABA BROOKS AND HIS
RECORDING BAND

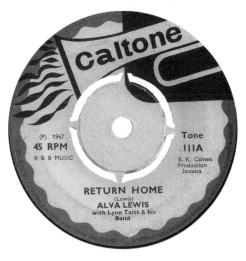

RETURN HOME
(Lewis)
ALVA LEWIS
with Lynn Taitt & his
Band

Chapter 5 Studio Time... First Session

I started in the record business for myself in 1967 but before that I used to be a record plugger... I'd take Beverley's, Duke Reid's and Coxsone's records and go to the radio stations to get them played. Incidentally it was Duke Reid started me in the business. He gave me my first studio time for free so that I could start doing my own sessions. I had twenty pounds and Lyn Taitt[1]. and Gladdy[2] took it and Duke Reid gave me the studio time because Duke was so pleased with what I'd done with 'Baba Boom'[3].

---

[1] Lyn Taitt: Born San Fernando, Trinidad 22nd June 1934 Nearlin 'Lyn' Taitt began his musical career when he was *"eight or nine years old"* as a steel pan player but, at the age of fifteen, he acquired a guitar which he first played in a group called The Dutchy Brothers. After two years Lyn left to form his own group who in 1962 were given a contract by Byron Lee to travel to Jamaica to play at the Independence celebrations. Lyn decided to stay in Jamaica and joined The Sheiks and then The Cavaliers playing at school dances and functions before forming Lyn Taitt & The Comets who continued to play live dates and also began to record as a band. Lyn had already recorded as a session guitarist and his first hit recording was 'Shank I Sheck' with Baba Brooks and his band in 1965. Lyn Taitt & The Jets came together in 1966 after signing to Federal Records on the strength of their leader's transcendent musical abilities. Lyn Taitt & The Jets rapidly became famous through their beautiful rock steady rhythms but Lyn began to feel the pressure of life as an outsider. It was inevitable that his incredible popularity could not come without a degree of envy and he was jealously referred to as a foreigner. In 1968, after two years of unprecedented and unparalleled musical creativity, Lyn was offered a contract to work as musical arranger for the house band at The West Indian Federated Club in Toronto, Canada. He *"jumped at the chance"* and left Jamaica in August never to return. Lyn Taitt died in Toronto, Canada 20th January 2010

[2] Gladdy: Gladstone 'Gladdy' Anderson: keyboards and musical arranger
[3] 'Baba Boom' – The Jamaicans – Treasure Isle (Jamaica & UK TI 7012) 7" 1967
"I had a lot of fun with Duke Reid. When we recorded the song 'Baba Boom' he gave us a crate of soft drinks. This was a big thing and we thought the Duke must really like us. We never knew about royalties. We just wanted girls..." Tommy Cowan of The Jamaicans

It won the Festival Song Competition[1] because Desmond Dekker should have won[2] and 'Baba Boom' won so Duke was pleased and he gave me the studio time and that was when I left KIG.

The first set of tunes I did was with Lyn Taitt... the greatest man that came to Jamaica and changed the whole beat from ska to rock steady was from Trinidad. Byron Lee did bring him come to Jamaica as an organist but he started playing guitar and the rest is history!

One of the biggest tunes he played on was 'Every Night'[3] for Mrs Pottinger[4] when she started. Ernest Ranglin[5] good you know but I'd say in **our** music the godfather of the rock steady come right on is Lyn Taitt. Rock steady... even now people record the one drop and it's rock steady man... we should call Lyn Taitt rock steady... it's not Ernest Ranglin... it's Lyn Taitt as he was the man! He played lead guitar and ska at the same time... he was very good. He was only on the island for a few years but they have a way in Jamaica if you get too good they pressure you... the musicians union... and you have to leave. Lyn Taitt is a great musician but they used politics to get him out... his work permit. That's why he ended up in Canada 'cause Lyn Taitt came as a foreigner and took over the whole music business. You think it's England alone deport people? Jamaica do a lot of that man!

---

[1] The Jamaican Cultural Development Commission Annual Festival Of The Arts was established in 1963 in the wake of the island's independence in order to *"develop and promote the creative talents and cultural expressions of the Jamaican people... also to ensure that the nation's cultural heritage is preserved for the benefit of future generations"*. Since its inception in 1966 the Song Contest proved to be the most popular aspect of the Festival and the Contest was the first step in the careers of many singers, songwriters and producers. In 1967 Desmond Dekker And The Aces came second with 'Unity' to the runaway winners: Tommy Cowan's Jamaicans with 'Baba Boom' for Duke Reid's Treasure Isle label

[2] 'Unity' – Desmond Dekker & The Aces – Beverley's (Jamaica)/Pyramid (UK) PYR 6017 7" 1967
*"It must be noted that the Festival Song Contest that year was rated as the best ever... mainly because of the rivalry of the artists! It was like a political campaign... artists had t-shirts advertising their songs & motorcades too! The winner was the Jamaicans' 'Baba Boom'... just edging out Desmond Dekker & The Aces' 'Unity'"*Derrick Harriott

[3] 'Every Night' - Joe White & Chuck Joseph/'1st Session' – Baba Brooks
- Gay Feet (Jamaica)/Doctor Bird DB 1001 (UK) 7" 1965
[4] Mrs Pottinger: Sonia Pottinger. Born 21st June 1931 Died 3rd November 2010. Proprietor of Tip Top record shop and record producer. Her labels included Gay Feet, High Note & Rainbow
[5] Ernest Ranglin: Supremely talented jazz guitarist and musical arranger for countless ska, rock steady and reggae records

Lyn Taitt & The Jets... but they changed that from Lyn Taitt & The Comets. He was a nice person too because when I started my thing I only had twenty pounds to give to Lyn Taitt and he got a four piece band. Himself and three others[1] and we did 'Music Field' with Roy Shirley[2], an Alva Lewis tune... 'I'm Going Home'[3] and a tune named 'Do It To Me Baby' with Lloyd & The Groovers[4] (sings) *"Isn't it good to hear the sound of music..."* and Derrick Morgan talked in it. Derrick was the man who helped me with the session... but we couldn't put his name on the label because he was still under contract to Beverley's. I used to move with Slim Smith and Derrick Morgan and Roy Shirley... by the way Roy Shirley was a big influence... and I started doing my own thing with them in the music.

So those guys helped me when I just started. I did about four tunes on that session and some of those tunes came out on Caltone 'cause I never had the money to put them out. After Duke had given me the studio time and I'd made the records I couldn't afford to cut the stamper so I had to give them to Caltone to put them out... I gave 'Do It To Me Baby' to Ken Lack because I didn't have no money to put out the record. I also gave WIRL[5] some to put out too. My brother, Don Lee, was working at WIRL as sales manager and he went to Mr Rae... Bunny Rae[6]... his right name was Clifford Rae but we used to call him Bunny Rae... an old army man. He always gave the little man a chance. He used to look out for us... gave us little producers studio time... cut our stampers and put out the records then they'd draw back their money. WIRL's sister company was in Barbados[7] so Mr Rae gave all of us a lot of chances and Mr Rae took 'Music Field' and put it out. It came out on Lee... I made a label named Lee first.

---

[1] Lyn Taitt: rhythm & lead guitar, Bryan Atkinson: bass, Joe Isaacs: drums and Gladstone 'Gladdy' Anderson: piano

[2] 'Music Field' – Roy Shirley – Lee/WIRL (Jamaica)/Doctor Bird DB 1093 (UK) 7" 1967

[3] 'Return Home' – Alva 'Reggie' Lewis – Caltone ((Jamaica & UK TONE 111) 7" 1967

[4] 'Do It To Me Baby' - Lloyd & The Groovers – Caltone ((Jamaica & UK TONE 108) 7" 1967

[5] WIRL: West Indies Records Limited, 13/15 Bell Road, Kingston 11

[6] Clifford 'Bunny' Rae: manager at West Indies Records Limited

[7] West Indies Records (Barbados) Limited: Applewhaites Estate, St Thomas, Barbados

Bunny 'Striker' Lee and Friends in Port Henderson

FAB

Copyright
Control

45 R.P.M.
(45/FAB 4IB)
FAB 4I
℗ 1968

RIDE YOU DONKEY
(C. Campbell, Tenners)
TENNERS
FAB RECORDS
LONDON
MADE IN ENGLAND

LET ME GO GIRL

45 R.P.M.

island
RECORDS

WI-3086
(A)

UNIQUES
Produced by: BUNNIE LEE
℗ 1967

LEE'S

10 East Ave.,
Kingston 13

MY CONVERSATION
THE UNIQUES

Gala

GALA 4001

THE TECHNIQUES
I'M SO IN LOVE
WITH YOU
(Franklyn White)

coxsone
RECORDS

℗ 1967

CS 7034
CSMX 5044 B

I'LL NEVER LET GO
SLIM SMITH
Produced by: COXSON DODD

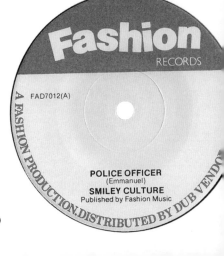

Fashion
RECORDS

A FASHION PRODUCTION.DISTRIBUTED BY DUB VENDOR

FAD7012(A)

POLICE OFFICER
(Emmanuel)
SMILEY CULTURE
Published by Fashion Music

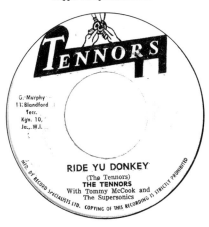

Chapter 6 Patient Man Ride Donkey

Seymour Stereo could build amplifiers probably even better than Tubbys, you know, 'cause Stereo was an engineer at a bauxite company and he was an electronics wizard. Stereo built his own amplifier... because if I was building a sound I would make Stereo do it because he was so good. There was a contest with Ruddys and Stereo in Spanish Town in 1967 and this is how so much people got to know about me.... he beat Ruddys that night and that's what really got me popular in the record business.

Now Coxsone and Duke Reid as the men of the day were backing Ruddys... all the other producers were backing Ruddys. So Stereo was the little guy and he came to me and said he wanted some help. *"Boy! Ruddys knows Duke Reid and Coxsone..."* so I said *"You'll have to rely on us!"* so we started making some specials, some super specials, with Val Bennett and some guys named The Tennors[1]. Clive Murphy had just cut a tune named 'Ride Yu Donkey'[2] and it had a wicked bass line and I asked him for a cut of it on soft wax for the contest and gave it to Stereo. And on the night of the dance I carried my crew of singers to sing 'pon him sound... Slim Smith and Roy Shirley... and they sang live on the sound. First time in history!

So on the night of that dance I took over my singers and Val Bennett and the specials we had made and the big sound system owners and record producers of

---

[1] The Tennors: renowned vocal trio, George 'Clive' Murphy, Maurice 'Professor' Johnson & Norman Davis, whose biggest hits were 'Pressure & The Slide'/'Pressure & Slide' -Studio One (Jamaica)/Coxsone CS 7024 (UK) 7" 1967 and 'Ride Yu Donkey' (see below) Ronnie Davis joined the group in 1968
[2] 'Ride Yu Donkey' – The Tennors – Tennors (Jamaica) 7" 1967

the day were backing Ruddys as Ruddys showed the way. So we went over with my crew and Slim Smith singing on the mic. and our specials but the tune that really put the icing on the cake that night… with all the big sound people there, you know… was 'Ride Yu Donkey'. Stereo could build amplifiers good and his sound was the heaviest so he put on (sings) *"When I was but a little laddie (my daddy bought a fiddle for me) and the only tune that I could play (yes sir) was 'Ride Me Donkey'"* and they crowned Stereo that night over this. The people went mad man! It had to play about twenty odd times. Stereo really knocked out Ruddy that night…

That backing became famous and 'Ride Yu Donkey' was an instant hit 'cause from that everyone wanted it. That tune sold like hot bread… big radio play… every sound man wanted it and the rest is history.

Prince Buster gave 'Ride Yu Donkey' to Emil Shallit[1] to release in England and Shallit put it out[2] and never paid Clive Murphy… The Tennors never got a penny out of it. So when I came up to England the following year I negotiated with Island. They gave The Tennors £250 and then they released it[3]. Because I gave it to Island and I carried Murphy's cheque up till now me and Murphy of The Tennors are friends for life. He lives in Miami now and we always talk about them things. I heard him and Monty Morris have got together and put out an album but I haven't seen it… some long time Treasure Isle and Prince Buster tunes on it.

So everybody started coming to me now… and then Mr Rae called me to do some more production because their in-house producer wasn't doing well. At that time it was Lee Perry so I went down there and I said to the boss we're going to have a session and make some tunes with Slim Smith and he said *"Yes!"* I had money to hire people because the company was paying for it so I had got Lyn Taitt and Tommy McCook and all the big musicians at that moment and we did this session 'Let Me Go Girl' with Slim Smith[4]. So when the session started we did a tune first with a girl named Beverley Simmons but I don't remember the song now[5]… When we did the Slim Smith tune Lee Perry came and set about the musicians: *"I'm the producer for the house and I don't know nothing about it!"* so the musicians started to panic and they came up to me as a newcomer and said *"How come you called us in the studio and Lee Perry and*

---

[1] Emil Shallit: proprietor of Melodisc Records, London. Melodisc's subsidiary labels included Blue Beat, Dice, Fab & Prince Buster

[2] 'Ride You Donkey' – The Tenners – FAB FAB 41 (UK) 7" 1968

[3] 'Ride Your Donkey' – The Tenners – Island WI 3133 (UK) 7" 1968

[4] 'Let Me Go Girl' – The Uniques – Lee (Jamaica)/Island WI 3086 (UK) 7" 1967

[5] 'Please Don't Leave Me' – Beverley Simmons – Lee's (Jamaica)/Island WI 3121 (UK) 7" 1968

them don't know about it?" I said *"The boss asked me to do it. I don't know because Lee Perry used to work between WIRL and Coxsone's studio and I'm just doing my work."*

Roy Shirley was supposed to sing next and he didn't sing so they followed me, the whole set of musicians, up with me to Mr Rae's office and the boss said *"What is this gentlemen? A strike?"* and they said *"No. This youth here come and say he's recording for West Indies Records and Lee Perry say him know nothing about it and stopped the session. We've done two songs already and we don't know if we're going to get paid."* So Mr Rae said *"I authorised with Bunny to go and do some things for us because anything we're doing with Lee Perry we're not making any money. His song 'Music Field' is Number Five in the chart."* So after that now Mr Rae said *"Alright gentlemen?"* and they decided to carry on with the session but I said *"No. You see how the beat's gone? The beat's gone already and I'm no longer in the mood. We're going to call it a day"* and we just settled for 'Let Me Go Girl'.

So Mr Rae paid them... and they fired Lee Perry 'pon the spot. I don't know if Roy Shirley had a hand in it too because he said *"Lee Perry took away my tune and went to Coxsone and Coxsone copied it"* [1] and told them that any time anyone did a tune at WIRL Lee Perry carried it up to Coxsone to let Coxsone hear it. So Mr Rae fired Scratch[2] and I became the in-house producer at WIRL. Roy Shirley is a great artist. He's a comedian! He has a style (sings) *"Again now get on the ball now friend... you've got to feel nice"* [3]. It was like comedy! He had a good voice and was like Oliver Samuels[4] Did you ever see Roy Shirley on stage? Him alright though... Roy Shirley. They used to have some guys in Jamaica imitating him who used to go down well with the crowd too. Yeah man...

And the next time I went down to voice a tune that's how The Uniques started. Because Slim Smith was a part of a group with Winston Riley[5] named The

---

[1] 'Hold Them' – Roy Shirley – Amalgamated & Jogibs (Jamaica)/Doctor Bird DB 1068 (UK) 7" 1967. Coxsone's version of the song was entitled 'Feel Good' – Ken Boothe – Studio One (Jamaica & UK SO 2000) 7" 1967

[2] Scratch: Lee 'Scratch' Perry

[3] 'Get On The Ball' – Roy Shirley – Caltone (Jamaica & UK TONE 101) 7" 1967

[4] Oliver Samuels: popular Jamaican comedian

[5] Winston Riley: Winston Riley formed The Techniques in 1962 at Kingston Senior School and at Chocomo Lawn Youth Club with original members Winston Riley, Keith 'Slim' Smith, Frederick Waite and Franklyn White. Pat Kelly, Junior Menz, Jackie Parris, Bobby Davis, Bruce Ruffin, Jimmy Riley, Dave Barker, Lloyd Parks, Morvin Brooks and Johnny from Johnny & The Attractions all later played their part in this multi talented group. Winston would go on to become one of Jamaica's most successful singers, record producers and record shop proprietors

Techniques and I said *"I'm going to form my own group named The Uniques"* and Keithy[1] also used to sing with The Sensations. The first Uniques was Derrick Morgan, Ken Boothe and Slim Smith... they sung the harmonies on (sings) *"People get ready to do rock steady..."* [2] that's the first Uniques tune. But the second one that mashed up the place was 'Let Me Go Girl' and BB Seaton and Lloyd Charmers[3] were singing on that one... and when the tune came out it was the baddest tune for 1967... it became a monster hit everywhere in Jamaica! Lynford 'Andy Capp' Anderson mixed and mastered it. You know (sings) *"Girl you hold me trying to control me..."* Then we did a Dawn Penn piece like it was the answer to it (sings) *"Boy me never hold you..."*[4] and then we did a Delroy Wilson tune named 'This Heart Of Mine'[5] where Ansel Collins[6] played drums.

So the Uniques officially were Slim Smith and Lloyd Charmers and the original 'My Conversation'[7] was just Slim Smith and Lloyd Charmers. When I formed the Uniques Jimmy Riley[8] wasn't in it... Lloyd Charmers did bring him in it. Jimmy Riley used to work at a bauxite company and him and Charmers were friends.

Winston Grennan played the piano on 'My Conversation'. He played the drum on the rhythm track because after Lyn Taitt I started to work with Bobby Aitken & The Carib Beats. So Winston Grennan was the drummer with the *"ding a ling"* piano on the voice track[9] and sometimes he made mistakes but I make it go same way! If a man made a mistake the whole thing would have to start over back again. Merritone[10]... he was a top sound man... our favourite sound system... like our radio station. Everybody used to follow Merritone so anything they played the other sounds would want it. Merritone loved it... they boosted it and people liked it and it became a classic all now... it's even been

---

[1] Keithy: Keith 'Keithy'/'Slim' Smith Born 1948. Died 1973
[2] 'People Rock Steady' – The Uniques – Lee's (Jamaica)/Island WI 3070 (UK) 7" 1967
[3] Lloyd Charmers: Lloyd 'Charmers' Tyrell gained his name from his hit making years in the early Sixties as one of The Charmers vocal duo alongside Roy Willis. He went on to become a member of The Uniques, a solo artist, musician and singularly successful record producer
[4] 'I'll Let You Go' – Dawn Penn – Lee (Jamaica)/Island WI 3097 (UK) 7" 1967
[5] 'This Heart Of Mine' – Delroy Wilson – WIRL (Jamaica)/Island WI 3099 (UK) 7" 1967
[6] Ansel Collins: keyboards & musical arranger
[7] 'My Conversation' – The Uniques – Lee's (Jamaica)/Island WI 3122 (UK) 7" 1968
[8] Jimmy Riley: Martin James 'Jimmy' Norman Riley: singer
[9] Winston Grennan: Born 16th September 1940. Died 27th October 2000. Winston Grennan played the drums with the other musicians as they laid the rhythm track and the piano part was then overdubbed onto the vocal track: *"when Slim and Charmers were voicing it him start fiddle around on the piano. I said leave him! Him have an idea... make it work. So that piano thing is in the voice track on the original"* Bunny 'Striker' Lee
[10] Merritone: Winston 'Merritone' Blake popular sound system controller and record producer

versioned more than 'Never Let Go'[1]. You know the two most versioned songs in whole reggae business? 'My Conversation' with Slim Smith and the tune they call 'I'll Never Let You Go' with Slim Smith. I have a version and Coxsone has a version of that tune. Every era they do it over and even Dub Vendor did have a tune named 'Producer' 'pon that rhythm. I think it went in the British Charts[2]. It was Beres Hammond's[3] biggest tune up till now... I think it's named 'Sweetness' or 'Niceness'[4] and it's there 'pon the 'My Conversation' rhythm. Shaggy's[5] there 'pon it too! Everybody's on the 'My Conversation' rhythm.

Every singer that you can think of has a piece of 'My Conversation'... that's another story again! Jimmy Riley sold the tape to Rupie Edwards[6]. Lloyd Charmers did an LP and asked me for it so I gave it to him and he added a three part harmony to it. That's the only time Jimmy Riley's in 'My Conversation'!

I started with Lyn Taitt but then everybody used him and Lyn Taitt started getting expensive. He remained my friend but he was so in demand that I then worked with a guy named Bobby Aitken and The Carib Beats[7] and I did 'My Conversation' and all them things with them. I had to record with Bobby because I couldn't afford Lyn Taitt although he was the man who started me off. I'd gave him and Gladdy twenty pounds and the studio time that Duke gave me but after that session those guys got a lot dearer. Those days it was thirty shillings[8] a side... if a man turned up you had to give him thirty shillings. So if you had ten men in the studio it was expensive and the stampers and all those things were expensive too. You just had to do your own thing to stay in the business. Old time people in Jamaica say *"Patient man ride donkey"* [9] and from that there was no looking back. Pure hits!

---

[1] 'I'll Never Let Go' – Slim Smith – Up Town (Jamaica)/Coxsone CS 7034 (UK) 7" 1967

[2] 'Police Officer' - Smiley Culture – Fashion FAD 26 12" & FAD 7012 7" 1985 A Number Twelve UK hit

[3] Beres Hammond: the most consistently successful Jamaican vocalist of the Nineties

[4] 'I Wish' – Beres Hammond – Signet (Jamaica) 7" 1993

[5] 'Give Thanks & Praises' - 'Pure Pleasure' – Shaggy - Greensleeves GREL 184 (UK) LP 1993

[6] Rupie Edwards: Rupert 'Rupie' Lloyd Edwards: record shop proprietor, vocalist and record producer Rupie subsequently used the 'My Conversation' rhythm for 'Yamaha Skank' - Pre Release (Jamaica) LP 1974. The first ever one rhythm album, memorably described as *"reggae's first concept album"*, the set featured the original vocal and eleven different instrumental and deejay interpretations of Striker's original 'My Conversation' rhythm

[7] Bobby Aitken & The Carib Beats: Bass: Vincent White Drums: Winston Grennan Guitar: Bobby Aitken Piano: Bobby Kalphat Organ: Ansel Collins

[8] Thirty shillings: £1.50

[9] *"Patient man ride donkey*: we must exercise great patience in order to reach our goals

A Patient Man

47

Chapter 7 Going International

If you cut me I'll cut you... but it's the same colour blood comes out. So I don't see the colour barrier in reggae music or any other music. It knows no colour. It comes like water. What colour would you call water now? Pure!

Benny King[1] came to Jamaica and started to acquire some tunes... Benny came but Rita stayed at home. Ken Lack was dealing with Benny... he was little man... but Mrs King was like a bully! She'd get on Benny's case and he'd do the running... they used to put Coxsone's stuff out up here. If Rita wasn't selling your record when it came out forget it! She'd call up Island and say *"I'm not selling any more* (of your records) *unless this or that tune reaches me!"* Dave Betteridge[2] and those guys at Island jumped quick! Yeah man. Rita used to call the shots. Benny used to come to Jamaica and we'd give him our tunes and he used to deal with Ken Lack a lot. Ken Lack put out 'Do It To Me Baby' and it caused a problem when I started with Island because Graeme Goodall[3] always put out music from West Indies Records on the Doctor Bird label in the UK and I'd put out 'Music Field' on WIRL. WIRL used to give Doctor Bird

---

[1] Rita & Benny King: Rita & Benny Isen (the pair anglicised their surname to King) were the proprietors of R & B Discs (for Rita & Benny), 282B Stamford Hill, London N16 a record shop founded in 1959. They also licensed and distributed Jamaican recordings in the UK initially on their R&B & Ska Beat labels and also on Caltone, Domain, Giant, Jolly, Hillcrest, Moodisc, Port O Jam & Sound System labels in the Sixties and early Seventies

[2] Dave Betteridge: *"Chris Blackwell's right hand man in the fast growing company..."*

[3] Graeme Goodall: legendary Kingston based Australian recording engineer

their things to put out and if a thing came out on WIRL in Jamaica then Doctor Bird[1] would automatically pick it up in the UK.

I met Dave Betteridge when he came to Jamaica and he heard the type of music I was doing... one day I was in the studio and Roy Shirley come and tell me a white man come from England was looking for me. Chris Blackwell is a great producer too, you know. I know Chris from before he ever broke big and I worked closely with Chris and Dave Betteridge. I used to ring them with what was happening in Jamaica. They wanted music to put out because at that time Island had got themselves Jamaican and soul tunes on the Sue label but they wanted more Jamaican music[2].

I first came up here in February 1968. England was a place where people could leave their milk and bread on the doorstep... when I first came I saw a cart and the man was delivering milk and bread and leaving it on the doorsteps. People in England were honest. It was a nice clean country. If a man could put down bread in your doorway it means the place must be clean! Yeah! England used to be a nice place! I came to see Dave Betteridge at Island when they were at 108 Cambridge Road... he'd sent me an invitation letter and when I came I brought up the tunes. He went to give me money and I said *"No man. Better you give me some instruments!"* and he bought me a set of instruments that I carried down. Bobby Aitken got a Gretsch guitar, Reggie[3] got a Gibson guitar I think, and some little Hofner bass like the Beatles used to play[4]. When Bobby Aitken started they used to make their own instruments. These guys couldn't afford to buy a guitar so when I carried back guitars and amplifiers for them they were glad 'cause now that Bobby Aitken had the Gretsch guitar he could get competitive with Lyn Taitt. Bobby Aitken had made his own guitar and Robbie Shakespeare[5] learnt to play off of Family Man on the little guitar like The Beatles used to have which was the bass we played on Pat Kelly's 'How Long'[6] and all those songs.

I carried back instruments for all my musicians and every man had his own instrument... one of the first tunes on that session[7] was 'Take Five'[8] in rock steady. We did over 'Take Five' and we were going to do it in the jazz form but

---

[1] Doctor Bird: Graeme Goodall's London based UK label
[2] Island Records released over sixty Bunny Lee productions during 1967 and 1968
[3] Reggie: Alva 'Reggie' Lewis: guitar
[4] Paul McCartney's Hofner Violin bass guitar
[5] Robert 'Robbie' Shakespeare: bass
[6] 'How Long' – Pat Kelly – Pama (Jamaica)/Gas GAS 115 (UK) 7" 1969
[7] The first recording session after Bunny had returned to Kingston
[8] 'Take Five' – Dave Brubeck Quartet - Fontana (UK) 7" 1961

I said *"No man. Make we rock it! Any tune can rock"* and Bobby Aitken and the bass went *"boom, boom, boom"* and slowed it right down. Winston Grennan was the drummer and we tried it. One cut! There was a comedy film called 'The Russians Are Coming'[1] that was popular at the time and when 'The Russians Are Coming'[2] came out it changed the whole business. It brought back instrumentals and all that because everyone had stopped using wind instruments in the rock steady. It was only Duke Reid who still used them. They were cutting down the expense and a man would use his guitar to play what the horns used to play. The horns man were getting hungry because they were not getting any work so I called them up now and made them do their own arrangements over the rock steady rhythms so you had plenty of instrumentals up to this day. You understand? I tried to keep instrumentals alive…

We used to listen to a lot of the American blues when I was growing up you know… so we used to copy the American blues. Plenty of those tunes that I make were from those tunes or some horn phrase that I remembered … 'Big Jay Shuffle' by Big Jay McNeely[3]… 'Page Boy Shuffle' by Joe Thomas[4] all those tunes there. I said to Val Bennett (sings) *"Boom ba boom ba badda boom…"* just do your own thing from now! But the musicians were young and they couldn't handle it. So I just changed it… the musicians couldn't get it so we called it 'Jumping With Val'[5] and they'd go into their own thing from that but it's really a take off of 'Page Boy Shuffle'. That was way down in the Sixties… '67 or '68. You used to have these old time musicians like Val Bennett and those men. In his day Val Bennett was a Louis Jordan fan… playing 'Caldonia'[6] and all those tunes. He and another man named Caldonia Robinson used to represent Louis Jordan in Jamaica. And we were in the studio and I feel I must make back some of those tunes because I used to like them so we started but somehow the flavour wasn't there. It was too boogieish and we wanted it more like ska… so we worked out something and we called that one 'Jumping With Val'.

You had some other ones too! One was 'Jumping With Mr Lee'[7]… Island put out an album[8] with it on… we did it with like a live effect on it and everybody

---

[1] 'The Russians Are Coming, The Russians Are Coming': A 1966 comedy film directed by Norman Jewison starring Alan Arkin, Carl Reiner & Eva Marie Saint
[2] 'The Russians Are Coming' – Val Bennett – Lee's (Jamaica)/Island WI 3146 (UK) 7" 1968
[3] 'Big Jay Shuffle' – Big Jay McNeely – Federal (USA) 10" 78rpm 1952
[4] 'Page Boy Shuffle' – Joe Thomas – King (USA) 10" 78rpm 1949
[5] 'Jumping With Val' – Val Bennett – Lee's (Jamaica)/Giant GN 34 (UK) 7" 1968
[6] 'Caldonia' – Louis Jordan & His Tympany Five – Decca (USA) 10" 78rpm 1945
[7] 'Jumping With Mr. Lee' – Val Bennett – Lee's (Jamaica)/Island WI 3113 (UK) 7" 1968
"Now ladies and gentlemen we are introducing to you the greatest man in tenor… Mr Val Bennett!"
[8] 'Leaping With Mr Lee' - Various Artists – Island ILP 986 (UK) LP 1968

in the studio shouted and clapped. I did it over with Tommy McCook because, after a while, I did a lot of work with Tommy McCook. At that time the other guys were claiming making instrumentals was too dear and I recorded a lot of the horns man in those days... Tommy McCook, Roland Alphonso, Lennox Brown and all those guys. You understand?

'Jumping With Mr Lee'... (sings) *"tump na nada, tump na nada"* was a tune named 'Hope, Skip & Jump'[1].... Lynn Hope did play that... and we made noise in the studio like a live effect and Val did vibes it up... *"blow man blow!"* So that was 'Jumping With Mr Lee' and Blackbeard[2] did bawl out (sings) *"Jumping with Mr Lee... tump na nada, tump na nada tump na nada, tump na nada tump"* but it never really worked out. 'Cause 'Page Boy Shuffle' and them things I think it's a tenor or a baritone sax did play... 'Hope, Skip & Jump' Val did use an alto sax or something. So he didn't get it right like the other one... it's similar but if you know the original one... well... you understand?

Louis Jordan had a tune named 'Pine Top's Boogie' right[3]? Tommy McCook and me did over the tune. I might look out the tape one day. That tune there is like jazz ska. Did you ever hear Louis Jordan's 'Pine Top's Boogie'? Those tunes keep the bass soprano beat. Even the owner didn't know the right guy or the name of the tune because the label was scratched off. Like *"I'm a country boy looking for a country girl...* there was about three of that song that were hits and then he found the woman and she said *"I'm your wife darling. You're going to mind me... now that you're married you have to mind me for the rest of your life... or to the jailhouse you go."* It was a rhythm & blues... a kind of half time tune and the sax work on it... the tenor or the alto sax... was marvellous. So any time you hear those tunes (sings) *"Ta na naaa..."* [4] the old time dancers like Sparky and all those people they loved it! All those tunes that you hear U Roy do are quotes from the old American blues records... all of them songs a man take out piece, piece of it and use it.

You have a tune... I don't get to do it yet but now most of these tenor sax guys are gone... it's only Dean Fraser[5] who you have now... (sings) *"I love you my darling more than you will ever know..."* I never got round to do it. That is one

---

[1] 'Hope, Skip & Jump' – Lynn Hope & His Orchestra - Aladdin (USA) 10" 78rpm 1951

[2] Blackbeard: Roderick 'Blackbeard' Sinclair, Tapper Zukie's elder brother, would later manage Striker's record shop at 101 Orange Street and go on to become a successful, highly respected record producer

[3] 'Pine Top's Boogie Woogie' - Louis Jordan – Decca (USA) 78rpm 10" 1948

[4] Perhaps further, possibly even answer, versions to 'Country Boy' – Dave Bartholomew – De Luxe (USA) 78rpm 10" 1950 and 'Country Boy Goes Home' – Dave Bartholomew – Imperial (USA) 10" 78rpm 1950

[5] Dean Fraser: Dean 'Youth Sax' Fraser/Frazer: saxophone

of the top sound system tunes with King Edwards the Giant and Coxsone and all them sounds. The sax work on it is brilliant! So you still have a few! I have some 78rpm records from them times that I put on cassette and make the musicians listen to them but sometimes you can't give away all your ideas until you're there in the studio because if you give a man too much ideas you'll hear it on the street before yours. That's how them new guys work you know!

Do you know Ernie Freeman's 'Live It Up'[1]? A lot of tunes in Jamaica came off of that rhythm[2]. They cut off the label when it came and named it 'Beard Man Shuffle' 'cause the Rasta man used to like it... so plenty of these tunes from Jamaica have different names so sometimes when you see the original you won't know what it is. They just gave it their own name. Most of Coxsone's instrumentals are Mongo Santamaria[3]... most of those songs like 'Bridge View'[4], 'Phoenix City'[5] and all them songs that is not their right name but Coxsone gave them those names. Some of those songs they just named them after movies like 'Guns Of Navarone'[6] but all those tunes like 'Ska El Pussy Cat'[7]...

When I came to England in February 1968 Fatman helped me out and another sound man named King Dougal... and with my sound men friend like Fatman[8] we started to do our work and bring out the music. That time Fatman used to play a sound named Fanso's Hi Fi till he went on his own. Fanso's gone back to Jamaica now and Fatman started his own sound. I introduced him to Prince

---

[1] 'Live it Up' – Ernie Freeman – Imperial (USA) 7" 1959

[2] including 'Beard Man Ska' – Roland Alphonso & The Skatalites – Studio One (Jamaica)/Island WI 228 (UK) 7" 1965, 'Herb Man' – King Stitt & Andy Capp – Clandisc (Jamaica & UK CLA 207) 7", 'Phantom' – The Dynamites – Dynamite (Jamaica)/Clandisc CLA 219 7" (UK) 1970 & 'Rastaman Shuffle' – The Upsetters – Black Ark Disco Bum 12" (Jamaica) 1977

[3] Mongo Santamaria: Born 7th April 1917. Died 1st February 2003. Afro Cuban Latin jazz percussionist

[4] 'Bridge View' – Roland Alphonso – C&N (Jamaica)/Ska Beat JB 163 (UK) 7" 1964 originally 'Funny Money' – Mongo Santamaria & His Orchestra

[5] 'Phoenix City' – Roland Alphonso – Studio One (Jamaica)/Doctor Bird DB 1020 (UK) 7" 1965 originally 'Hammer Head' – Mongo Santamaria & His Orchestra

[6] 'Guns Of Navarone' – Roland Alphonso & The Studio 1 Orchestra – Musik City (Jamaica)/Island WI 168 (UK) 7" 1965 actually credits 'Dimitri, Tiomti & Paul Francis Webster as composers. The theme music to J. Lee Thompson's Second World War blockbuster film 'Guns Of Navarone' starring Gregory Peck, David Niven and Anthony Quinn was originally released as 'The Guns Of Navarone' – Joe Reisman Orchestra & Chorus – Landa (USA) 7" in 1961 credited to Dimitri Tiomkin & Paul Webster

[7] 'El Pussy Cat Ska' - Roland Alphonso & The Studio 1 Orchestra – Studio One (Jamaica)/Island WI 217 (UK) 7" 1965 originally 'El Pussy Cat' - Mongo Santamaria & His Orchestra

[8] Fatman: Ken 'Fatman' Gordon London based sound system controller, record shop proprietor and record producer

Jammy[1]... as he was that time... and Fatman brought up Jammy and they changed the whole sound system thing. When I came here they only had two or three controls... the most they'd have is four controls on a sound system. But Jammy built a complete pre-amp like a sound have in Jamaica and you could hear the separation... the treble at the top, the mid-range and the bass...so when you start playing a record you'd bring in the tops and the middle and then you'd just lick in the bass. It was awesome... it was different you know... so Fatman became the top sound system in the Seventies right on until the late Eighties. But in those days King Dougal and a sound named Sting Ray used to run over that side. Count Shelly used to have his sound and a few others. As you know Duke Vin was there too but Shelly's sound was popular.

And Clancy Collins[2]... Sir Collins and His Musical Wheel. We did 'Sir Collins Special' with Lester Sterling[3], a trombonist named Danny Sims and Lloyd Charmers doing the vocal over it on the Roy Shirley rhythm[4]. We recorded it in WIRL studio...

I was staying in the East End of London and that's why we did a tune called 'Forest Gate Rock'[5]... but it was a tune named 'Barbados'[6] that Charlie Parker did first. And then I hooked up with Pama[7]...

---

[1] Prince Jammy: Lloyd 'Prince Jammy' later 'King Jammy' James: sound system controller, recording engineer and record producer who would go on to establish Jammy's Recording Studio
[2] Clancy Collins: 'Sir Collins Down Beat' London based Jamaican sound system controller and record producer
[3] 'Sir Collins Special' – Lester Sterling – Sir Collins Down Beat CR 001 (UK) 7" 1967
[4] 'Music Field' – Roy Shirley – Lee/WIRL (Jamaica)/Doctor Bird DB 1093 (UK) 7" 1967
[5] 'Forest Gate Rock' – Lee's Blank Label (Jamaica)/Big Shot BI 506 (UK) 7" 1969
[6] 'Barbados' – Charlie Parker – Savoy (USA) 10" 78rpm 1948
[7] Pama Records Ltd., 16 Peterborough Road, Harrow, Middlesex and later 78 Craven Park Road, Harlesden, London NW10

Bunny 'Striker' Lee

Edward O'Connor Lee

Bunny 'Striker' Lee

Ruby May McGaw

Bobby Aitken

Clement 'Coxsone' Dodd

Roy Shirley

Bunny 'Striker' Lee

David Rodigan MBE and Bunny 'Striker' Lee OD

Bunny 'Striker' Lee

Bunny 'Striker' Lee, Brad Osborne and Friend, Clocktower Records, New York

The Uniques: Lloyd 'Charmers' Tyrell, Keith 'Slim' Smith and Jimmy Riley

Bunny 'Striker' Lee, 5 West Avenue, Greenwich Farm

Earl 'Chinna' Smith, Bunny 'Striker' Lee, Dennis Brown, Dave Lee and Friends in London

Delroy Wilson

John Holt

Annette Wong Lee and Bunny 'Striker' Lee 28th July 1990, Kingston

David Lee, Bunny 'Striker' Lee and Mark Lee

Bunny 'Striker' Lee and Annette Wong Lee at Clocktower Records

Peter Tosh, Bunny 'Striker' Lee and Friends, Rainbow Theatre, London

Roger Cargill, Bunny 'Striker' Lee, Leroy Smart and Fatman, Toronto

John Holt, Delroy Wilson, Dennis AlCapone and Bunny 'Striker' Lee

Ava Gill, Miss Jamaica 1971, and Bunny 'Striker' Lee

Slim Smith

Johnny Clarke

Bunny 'Striker' Lee

Count Shelly and Leroy Smart

Dennis AlCapone

Dennis AlCapone, Derrick Morgan, Jimmy Cliff and Bunny 'Striker' Lee

Horace Andy

Jah Stitch

WIRL Records

Lee 'Scratch' Perry

Bunny 'Striker' Lee

King Jammy at the controls

Augustus Pablo

Prince Jazzbo, Bunny 'Striker' Lee, Max Romeo and Max's children

Bunny 'Striker' Lee and Tapper Zukie

Bunny 'Striker' Lee and Lennox Lewis

Bunny 'Striker' Lee, Edward Seaga and Olivia 'Babsy' Grange

Stephen Marley, Bunny 'Striker' Lee and Ziggy Marley, Rainbow Theatre, London

Sly Dunbar, Jimmy Riley and Robbie Shakespeare

Lloyd Parks and Bunny 'Striker' Lee

Beverley
Music
(P) 1969

45
RPM

GAS 105B

ENGLISH TALK
A. Ellis
ALTON ELLIS
Alton & Johnny

PAMA
RECORDS

Palmer Music
© 1968

45 RPM
PM 717A

MY TIME IS THE RIGHT TIME
(Ellis)
ALTON ELLIS
Produced by Ellis/Moore

PAMA RECORDS LTD.
118 Orange St.
Upstairs
PHONE 22869

PAMA
RECORDS

Palma Music
PM 701A

45 RPM
℗ 1967

WHAT WILL YOUR MAMA SAY
(C. Eccles)
CLANCY ECCLES

DOCTOR BIRD

DB-1093 A
Island
Music

Wirl
℗ 1967

MUSIC FIELD
ROY SHIRLEY

45
RPM
PH 21 (1)

CLINT EASTWOOD
THE UPSETTERS

Pama Records London

Chapter 8 Boss Sounds On Pama... Records With The Best Beat

Pama Records started a little after when Trojan formed when Harry Palmer came to Jamaica and gave Clancy Eccles[1] some money. Alton Ellis got money from Pama too when he was in the UK with Coxsone[2] and Pama got some tunes from him[3]. When I first met them their real business was auctioneers and they used to buy and sell houses. I was staying with a friend in East London and one Sunday morning my friend said *"Bunny... three black men want to see you downstairs"*. They came up and we started to talk. Carl did all the talking... he was an expert on real estate... but he and Harry did a little record business on the side. They used to have a club named Thirty One and when they redeveloped the area they had to find a new place and they named it Apollo, you know, after the club in America[4]. I said: *"Call it Apollo. Yeah man"*... Jeffrey still runs it[5]. They used to say *"we're black men"* and they'd win you over.

I had started with Dave Betteridge at Island and a little after that Island and Blue Cat amalgamated and formed Trojan. Blue Cat had some Studio One things and some of Joe Gibbs' first things on Amalgamated. Joe Gibbs came up here in 1967 but he used to deal with Blue Cat... even though I brought him in the

---

[1] Clancy Eccles: Born 9th December 1940. Died 30th June 2005. Singer, record shop proprietor and record producer. 'What Will Your Mama Say' - Clancy Eccles - Pama PM 701 (UK) 7" 1967 was the second 7" release on the Pama label
[2] The Soul Vendors 1967 UK tour
[3] 'English Talk' – Alton Ellis Pama PM 707 (UK) 7" 1968
'My Time Is The Right Time' – Alton Ellis Pama PM 717 (UK) 7" 1968
[4] Apollo: Apollo Theater, Harlem, New York, USA
[5] The Apollo Club, 375 High Road, Willesden, London NW10

business Joe Gibbs had come to England before me and met Lee Gopthal[1]. One of the men who did a lot for this music but people don't talk about him was an Indian man called Lee Gopthal. Him and Desmond Bryan[2] and Webster Shrowder[3] used to go house to house you know... selling records from their little bags until they formed a thing with Joe Gibbs named Amalgamated. Island had the building on Cambridge Road and Lee Gopthal... who had Blue Cat with Webster Shrowder and those guys... and when they got this place with Blue Cat downstairs and with Island on the top they decided to amalgamate and call it Trojan after Duke Reid's label.

Duke was an independent man, you know, and Duke Reid's records used to do good up here but, because Duke used to wear his gun and things, Lee Gopthal and Dave Betteridge were afraid to face him. When Dave Betteridge came to Jamaica I carried him to Duke Reid... because I used to work with Duke I knew his temperament. We talked to Duke and he was agreeable and he said *"Well, alright"*. They decided to make the Trojan label for England because no one was releasing Duke's things but Duke was a wealthy man in Jamaica... he had a lot of trucks and dumpers away from his liquor business... so he didn't really need Trojan or anybody else to release his things. Duke is the original Trojan... Duke Reid The Trojan that's what his sound was named.

When I first came here in 1968 Dandy Livingstone[4] was working with Mrs King... Rita King... she used to pay him twenty pounds a week as a producer. Dandy did have a big hit with 'Rudy A Message To You'[5] but Rita and Dandy were having problems so the Palmer brothers gave Dandy money to make an album. But Dandy got to meet me when he was rehearsing and me and Dandy became good friends. I was going to Trojan afterwards. He was driving so he took me down there and Dandy sold them this album that Pama was supposed to get because Pama's money had made it!

---

[1] Lee Gopthal: Jamaican Indian Leichman 'Lee' Gopthal accountant and director of Beat & Commercial Records distribution, Trojan Records and the Musicland, later Muzik City, chain of record shops

[2] Desmond Bryan: director of the Muzik City chain of record shops, Trojan Records and later Klik Records

[3] Webster Shrowder: director of the Muzik City chain of record shops, Trojan Records and later Vulcan Records

[4] Dandy Livingstone: Robert 'Dandy Livingstone' Thompson London based Jamaican singer and record producer

[5] 'Rudy A Message To You' – Dandy & His Group – Ska Beat JB 273 (UK) 7" 1967

That was one of first albums that came out on Trojan. It was named 'Dandy Returns'[1]... you see him coming off of the steps of a plane. I remember Dave Betteridge was there on the 'phone and sold fifteen thousand of it!

Dandy told the Palmer brothers that me and him were cousins... *"No. He's my cousin"* so the Palmer brothers came round and had a talk. I was staying over East London and the three brothers came over there. I told them don't bother with the police and me and Dandy will come and see you and I will give you some tunes and we can work together. Then Dandy picked me up and took me to their office in Harrow where the Palmer brothers were in real estate. Even after what had happened they decided to have one more go at it so that evening they gave me seven hundred pounds... about four hundred pounds in cash and three hundred pounds in a cheque. I don't remember exactly... it might be vice versa. Harry said *"Oh it's so much money I'm giving these people!"* and I said *"It's not my money! It's you and your client's money"*. He left and went out of the office saying *"Well I want you to utilise it"*.

We decided to make a label with a black hand and a white hand shaking over a mountain named Unity and I went to Jamaica and I utilised that seven hundred pounds. With the money I made 'Bangarang'[2] and all that and Pama took over the whole entire business.

In them days if a man put a record out in England he'd get one hundred and fifty pounds ... that's coming like you'd get a hundred and fifty thousand now! You could buy a TV set... you could buy a bedroom suite... you could pay rent and go back to market. When I say go back to market I mean you had enough money to go back to the studio and make more records! In those days if a man got one hundred and fifty pounds from England it was big thing! You understand? Those days were cheaper but... you know. Every time I came from England I used to walk out of my gates and give people money... they never knew their tunes had been released in London... so that was a surprise for them!

The first time a record[3] played in their club if Jeffrey saw that the crowd liked it he'd put it up and in the middle of the night they'd play it again and if the crowd said *"Yeah!"* then they'd play it three times in the night. Jeffrey would say to the deejay: *'Smokey... you think that one could a sell?"* and on Monday he'd

---

[1] 'Dandy Returns' - Dandy – Trojan TRL2 (UK) LP 1968 was the second album to be released on Trojan. The first, 'Follow That Donkey' by The Brother Dan All Stars - Trojan TRL1 (UK) LP 1968), was also produced by Dandy
[2] Bangarang' – Lester Sterling & Stranger Cole
– Carifta & Lee's (Jamaica)/Unity UN 502 (UK) 7" 1968
[3] a record: a Jamaican pressed pre-release record

arrange to master it. Afro, another deejay, or Smokey Joe would master it. By the weekend it would be out on the street and in the shops. Sometimes Trojan would squeal *"but we have the contract"* and the two companies would put out the same tune. But at that time if a man got an advance his tune would come out and sell way past that because both Trojan and Pama had put it out. A lot of the time them little things did go on and by this time Mrs King was doing a lot less.

When their tunes came out Mr Palmer would give me money to carry back to the artists... when I'd come up from Jamaica I'd say *"Mr P? Them guys want some money"*. So I'd get a contract from them and go back down and give them the money so they got the deal and became the legal distributor. Sometimes Pama would put out the tune and call me and I'd tell the guys and they'd say *"well alright go ahead and send me the contract and I'll sign it"*. And Trojan did the same thing too with guys like Webster Shrowder. Other guys would just take up a record and cut it but Trojan and Pama would do it legally 'cause they'd put out the tunes and give me the money to carry back to the youths in Jamaica. They set up Pama Records in Jamaica[1] to take care of that afterwards and a man just got his advance right there so and done!

Carl is a clever business man... they did work for themselves too you know[2] and they're still in business all now. It named Jet Star[3] now. Harry's in Jamaica now. He has a church and every Sunday morning you can see him praying on the television on a station named CVM. He's a good church man and a good preacher too! And Jeffrey still runs the club and Carl is still in the record business with Jet Star.

So everybody used to look for me after Pama became the big thing. When I came up here I started to bring the little producers together and we'd give our tunes to Pama so they started to come up now. Harry J[4], everybody came and stayed with Pama in London. I said to Mr Palmer that me alone can't do it 'cause *"one hand can't clap"* [5] but I have a friend... that friend was Lee Perry.

---

[1] Pama Records Ltd. 118 Orange Street Upstairs, Kingston
[2] Pama produced their own soul and reggae recordings in London
[3] Jet Star Phonographics, 155 Acton Lane, Park Royal, London NW10
[4] Harry J: Harry 'Harry J' Johnson internationally successful record producer who would later establish the Harry J Recording Studio
[5] *"one hand can't clap"*: people must co-operate with each other in order to ensure the successful implementation of projects and activities

Duke Reid 'The Trojan'

Chapter 9 Scratch The Upsetter And Niney The Observer

When Scratch got fired from West Indies Records me and Scratch started to move because Scratch never have no money. Coxsone and him never got on and that's why he left for West Indies Records. Now he was nowhere. So then he used to come in the studio at night time and make his things because "*I no come to count cow. I came here to drink milk*" [1] … that's a saying.

I used to let Lee Perry come back and work at night time and do his own things so we became good friends and we started running sessions for one another and when me and Pama were working together I told Pama about him. Pama gave me five hundred pounds for him to start and I 'phoned him and him come and meet me at the airport and I just put the five hundred pounds in him hand. That's how the Upsetter label started and Pama started putting out his records until Scratch started to get rich and switch on his own. That's how the man got the money to start. Carl Palmer gave Scratch a Jaguar… not brand new… but in Jamaica if a guy a drives a Jaguar it was a big thing! And when he cleared it from the wharf Scratch drove it up and he put it in a purple colour[2] and started carrying a big briefcase so things started happening. You understand? So you see where the business is coming from? Me and Scratch did a whole heap of recording. We were inseparable. You see me you see Lee Perry… especially after Pama gave me that money to give him!

---

[1] "*I came here to drink milk, not to count cows*": mind your own business and enjoy what you are entitled to; do not worry about details which do not concern you
[2] put it in a purple colour: re-painted/re-sprayed the car purple

Me and Scratch were such good friends that we ran sessions 'pon the same tape... same set of musicians... they didn't know if it was my thing or Scratch's thing. For instance you know 'Shocks Of Mighty'[1] with Dave Barker? It's me who gave Lee Perry a cut of that rhythm. It was a tune named 'Hook Buttoo'[2] but we call it 'Buttoo Girl' and some other tunes go on that rhythm... 'Prisoner Of Love'[3] with Dave Barker... Lester Sterling blew an instrumental on it and Slim Smith sang a foreign tune named 'Slip Away'[4] on it. Ranny Bop[5] and Ansel Collins worked out the track with Niney[6]. That guy now... people don't talk about him... but we call him Ranny Bop. He was a very good musician. He played on the Duke Reid tunes... if it's not Hux Brown[7] it's him... he was part of Tommy McCook's[8] band. So he used to play with The Supersonics and he was an Aggrovator. He's the guy who used to tell Reggie and Glen[9] and Family Man[10] the chords. I don't know how they leave him out but through him go to Canada people tend to forget him but he made some great tunes. Ranny Bop used to live in England for a little while where he made 'Tenderly' with Ginger Williams[11]. He did a lot of tunes but people don't talk about him... 'Throw Me Corn'[12]... a lot of tunes. He lives in Canada now and he's a very good musician... but people forget him.

Scratch didn't want to give Niney a chance. He used to be working for Scratch and Clancy[13] and he didn't sell enough records but he liked the business and Scratch and Clancy were taking disadvantage of him. I said *"leave the youth man"* and he took a liking to me. When I first knew him he was a singer... him and a guy named Nehemiah[14]... and I said *"You can't do the youth like that man!"* and we took him over. *"You want to come and work for me?"* Niney was

---

[1] 'Shocks Of Mighty' – Dave Barker – Upsetter (Jamaica & UK US 331) 7" 1970

[2] 'Hook Buttoo'/'Buttoo Girl' – The Inspirations – Lee's Blank (Jamaica) 7" 1969

[3] 'Prisoner Of Love' – Dave Barker – Upsetter (Jamaica)/Punch PH 020 (UK) 7" 1969

[4] 'Slip Away' – Slim Smith – Unity Blank (Jamaica)/Unity UN 520 (UK) 7" 1970 originally 'Maybe We Can Slip Away' – Percy Sledge – Atlantic (USA) 7" 1967

[5] Ranny Bop: Lorraine 'Ranny Bop' Williams: guitar & musical arranger

[6] Niney: Winston 'Niney The Observer' Holness also known as George Boswell

[7] Hux Brown: Lynford 'Hux' Brown: guitar

[8] Tommy McCook's Band: Tommy McCook. Born 3rd March 1927. Died 5th May 1998. Tenor saxophone, band leader & hugely influential musical arranger at Treasure Isle studio for Duke Reid's house band Tommy McCook & The Supersonics

[9] Glen: Glenroy 'Glen'/'Capo' Adams: Born 27th November 1945. Died 18th December 2010. Keyboards, singer & musical arranger

[10] Family Man: Aston 'Family Man' Barrett: bass guitar

[11] 'I Can't Resist Your Tenderness' aka 'Tenderly' – Ginger Williams – Paradise PR 01 (UK) 7" 1975

[12] 'Throw Me Corn' – Winston Shand – Carib Dis Co (Jamaica)/Gas GAS 120 (UK) 7" 1969

[13] Clancy: Clancy Eccles

[14] Nehemiah: Nehemiah Reid

a salesman for me and so Niney became one of the best salesmen for Pama and myself in Jamaica. I bought him a bike and he'd go to every dance promoting the tune them until every sound man in Jamaica knew Niney. Niney started coming to the studio now and I want to tell you that one of the greatest rhythms that I have it's Niney make it: ... Niney was the man that came up with the bass lines for Slim Smith with 'Ain't Too Proud To Beg'[1] and 'Slip Away'... Niney! When I gave Scratch a cut of 'Slip Away' Scratch put Dave Barker on the rhythm with 'Prisoner Of Love' and that gave Niney a chance to branch off and start doing his own thing 'cause he's a very creative person.

Niney had plenty of ideas about the business. When I went to the studio I'd say *"Niney. Make Scratch and you see what you can do"* and we'd go into the studio with the musicians and the singers. Niney and Slim Smith were very good friends too and on 'Ain't Too Proud To Beg' I sat in the control booth and said *"Niney... Show them"*. Scratch was there too and Niney came up with the idea for the rhythm... Niney and Ansel Collins. So you have to say Niney started off producing with me but first of all he was a singer. Then he started working with Dennis Brown and you know the rest is history. One of Ken Boothe's best tunes up until now is Niney's 'Silver Words'[2]. Niney do a whole heap of things... Niney's part of the history of this thing... but he was brilliant as a salesman. He's a singer coming from selling the records, promoting the records, to his own productions when he started doing his own thing. Niney would come in the studio and I'd say: *"Niney. Take over..."* and him know what him doing!

Even to this day... we have our ups and downs... you understand? That's how 'Mr Chatterbox'[3] came out ... through Niney. Bob Marley and Bunny Wailer[4] had done a tune already for Coxsone named 'Mr Talkative'[5] so at the start of the 'Mr Chatterbox' record I said *"Bob so how the session work out? "'* and me and Bob a talk and me say *"Niney a come"* and Bob said *"him Mr Talkative that..."* When Bob Marley had his shop in King Street[6] where Jah Stitch[7] got shot I used to carry him records. We used to have contacts at the record pressers up at Chancery Lane and the press used to drop a hundred records off at my shop in

---

[1] 'Ain't Too Proud To Beg' – Slim Smith – Unity (Jamaica & UK UN 515) 7" 1969
also 'Too Proud To Beg' – The Uniques – Gas GAS 117 (UK) 7" 1969
[2] 'Silver Words' – Ken Boothe – Observer (Jamaica)/Green Door GD 4053 (UK) 7" 1973
[3] 'Mr Chatterbox' – Bob Marley – Agro Sounds Blank (Jamaica)/Jackpot JP 730 (UK) 7" 1970
Bunny 'Striker' Lee produced update of The Wailers' Studio One recording 'Mr Talkative'
[4] Bunny Wailer: Neville O'Riley 'Bunny Wailer' Livingston: one of the original Wailers
[5] 'Mr Talkative' – The Wailers – Coxsone (Jamaica)/Island WI 188 (UK) 7" 1963
[6] Wailers Records, 127 King Street, Kingston
[7] Jah Stitch: Melbourne 'Jah Stitch' James: deejay and later selector for Sugar Minott's Youth Promotion sound system in the Eighties

Orange Street and I've give Bob fifty or twenty five. Niney heard 'Blood & Fire'[1] in Bob's shop and when they told him they got it from me Niney started! Him say that Bob and myself went round to the press and took away his records. Bob did hear and so then Bob did come and challenge Niney right before the shop and Niney said *"Blood and fire, blood and fire"* and 'Blood & Fire' hit. I just said Niney loves to talk and so we decided to make the tune off a him. So it's *"Mr Chatterbox how long will you live?"*

Ainsley Folder was a man who looked after the pressing plants at Federal. He worked there for years... he got a cut of the 'Have Some Mercy'[2] rhythm from Lee Perry... it was a soul tune called 'I Forgot To Be Your Lover'[3]. You know Delroy just went into the studio and did a freelance thing 'pon it? But it wasn't really the vocal that sold that tune. It was the rhythm... when it was being mastered Niney fiddled with the controls and the people liked it. What really sell the tune was when it was mastered Niney was fiddling with it in the control room *"Skkkewwwiiii"* and that sound came out on the master but it wasn't on any tape. So if you wanted it now you'd have to run it off of the forty five and that carried that record man! You understand? Then Delroy came up to London and I had to tell him *"Delroy. Go back to Jamaica! The tune that you did for Ainsley Folder is mashing up the whole of Jamaica! Better you go down because you're in England a waste time and they need you down there for stage shows!"* Me and him voiced some tunes up here... that night there was a TV in the studio and Cassius Clay and Joe Frazier were fighting[4]. Then Delroy went back to Jamaica.

It was one of the biggest selling records in Jamaica but that rhythm have some jinx you know! Any artist who goes on it dies after a while! It was done first by Shenley Duffus[5] then George Faith[6] sung over the same tune, then Delroy Wilson[7], Jacob Miller[8], Augustus Pablo[9] did a cut for Ainsley Folder... all those

---

[1] 'Blood And Fire' – Niney – Observer (Jamaica)/Big Shot BI 568 (UK) 7" 1971
[2] 'Have Some Mercy' – Delroy Wilson – Dee Jay (Jamaica)/Cactus CT 22 (UK) 7" 1973/74
[3] 'I Forgot To Be Your Lover' - William Bell – Stax (USA) 7" 1968
[4] Muhammad Ali vs Joe Frazier Madison Square Garden, New York USA 28th January 1974
[5] 'To Be A Lover' – Shenley Duffus – Goodies (Jamaica)/Upsetter US 386 (UK) 7" 1972
Shenley Duffus Born 10th February 1938. Died 9th February 2002
[6] 'To Be A Lover' – George Earl (George Faith)
– Upsetter (Jamaica)/Mango MS 2015 (UK) 7" 1977 George Faith Born 1946. Died 23rd May 2003
[7] 'Have Some Mercy' – Delroy Wilson – Dee Jay (Jamaica) 1973/Cactus CT 22 (UK) 7" 1974
Delroy Wilson: Born 5th October 1948. Died 6th March 1995
[8] 'Have Some Mercy' –The Inner Circle featuring Jacob Miller
'Rock The Boat' – The Inner Circle – Trojan TRLS 93 (UK) LP 1974
Jacob Miller Born 4th May 1952. Died 23rd March 1980
[9] 'Pablo's Mercy' – Augustus Pablo – Deejay (Jamaica) 7" 1974
Horace 'Augustus Pablo' Swaby Born 21st June 1953. Died 18th May 1999

fellows died you know![1] I have a cut of the 'Have Some Mercy' rhythm on four track and Glen Washington[2] did ask me for a cut of the rhythm the other day. I said *"Glen. I'll give you the rhythm but this rhythm looks like it has a jinx. But if you feel you can break the jinx I'll tell you the history about it..."* I started telling him and he said he'd skip it!

I had a sound system in the Pama days but I gave it to the guys round Scratch and it became the Upsetter Sound. We'd bought this sound from Lloyd The Matador. I did want to buy a sound through Tubbys but 'cause Pama was dealing with Lloyd The Matador the man sold me a sound system and I challenged Mudies from Spanish Town 'cause Mudies was a big sound system man. He had a nice little club and he was a very good producer too. I challenged him that night and I said *"I'm going to kill you with music!"* When Mudies turned on his sound it made ours sound like... how they say... a zinc pan sound. So I lost interest right away! Heh, heh, heh. All the amplifiers catch a fire and started to burn up. Men like Lloyd The Matador were sound system men but they couldn't build sound systems. I was going to start back the sound but wanted to use Seymour Stereo to build the amplifier. When Tubbys built a sound... 16KT at the bottom a play bass and 10KT at the top... and Stereo built one with 10KT at the bottom and 6KT[3] at the top and when the guy played Tubbys in a contest Tubbys got burned up.

One time I was in England I sent Glen Adams the money to run a session for me at Coxsone's studio[4] with Scratch singing an American song *"I'm sick and tired of fooling around with you..."*[5]. Scratch put Val Bennett on it and made 'Return Of Django'[6]... that solo you hear playing is Val Bennett. Scratch sent up the tune to England and called it 'Return Of Django' through the 'Django' films with Franco Nero[7]. Those films take life in Jamaica! The tune took on and hit up here in England and when Tony Cousins came to Jamaica Scratch wanted to

---

[1] Pat 'Jah Lloyd'/'Jah Lion' Francis Born 29th August 1947. Died 2nd June 1999 was also given a cut of the rhythm by Lee Perry which he used extensively for his own productions on the Teem label including 'Soldier Round The Corner' – Jah Lloyd - Teem (Jamaica)/Dip DI 5021 (UK) 7" 1974 *"what a whole lot a versions of this rhythm a gwaan a street!"*
[2] Glen Washington: singer
[3] 16KT, 10KT & 6KT: amplifier valves
[4] Studio One, 13 Brentford Road, Kingston 5, Jamaica
[5] 'Sick And Tired' – Chris Kenner – Imperial (USA) 7" 1957
[6] 'Return of Django' – The Upsetters
– Upsetter (Jamaica & UK US 301) 7" 1969 A Number Five UK hit
[7] 'Django': a 1966 Italian spaghetti western, reputedly *"one of the most violent films ever made"*, directed by Sergio Corbucci and starring Franco Nero. Jimmy Cliff, as Ivan, watches the film at Kingston's Rialto cinema in 'The Harder They Come'. 'Django' proved so popular that other film makers appropriated the character's name for their films including Alberto de Martino's 'Django Shoots First' in 1966 and Osvaldo Civirani's 'Son Of Django'/'The Return Of Django' in 1967

carry Winston Wright and all those guys for the UK tour but I said *"No. It's my musicians that have to go..."* Carlie[1], Family Man, Glen Adams and Alva Lewis... who we called Reggie. So Scratch came on tour instead of Val Bennett and he got a horn player in England named Kirk to play his part. Val never forgave Scratch. I had paid him to play the song and he should have got the tour. Val Bennett was a bitter man over that up till his death.

Sometimes when music would be playing Scratch would come and rock, rock, rock 'pon the keyboard and I'd say *"Don't bother stop it!"* 'cause that sound good. It was madness... *"bwuummp, bwuumpp"*... and it became a part of the music. People say Scratch is crazy but that is his way of doing things. Because plenty of writers say he is a mad genius... and genius is mad but Scratch won't come and do any foolishness.

---

[1] Carlton 'Carlie' Barrett: Born 17th December 1950. Died 17th April 1987. Drums

Niney The Observer and Bunny 'Striker' Lee

UNITY
EXPORT ONLY
45 R.P.M.
UN 004 A
TEL. 22869
PAMA
TTC
1000 TONS OF MEGATON
(R. Alphonso)
ROLAND ALPHONSO
WITH THE BUNNY LEE ALL STARS
DISTRIBUTED BY UNITY RECORDS, 118 ORANGE ST., KGN. JA.

GAY FEET
DISTRIBUTED BY
TIP TOP RECORD
CENTRE
Unauthorised
Copying is
Prohibited
37 ORANGE ST.
KINGSTON
JAMAICA, W.I.
VOCAL
45 R.P.M.
S 132
THE WHIP
L. DILLON
THE ETHIOPIANS
LYN TAITT & THE JETS

BLUE BEAT
Copyright
Control
Recording first
published 1965
45/BB 324
(45/BB 3786A)
AL CAPONE
(C. Campbell)
PRINCE BUSTER'S ALL STARS
MELODISC RECORDS
LTD.

COXSONE
RECORDS
C 112
MR. TALKETIVE
THE WAILERS
MANUFACTURED BY FEDERAL RECORD MFG. CO. LTD. JAMAICA W.I.

UPSETTER
B&C/Island
Music
US-301 A
TMX.73
RETURN OF
DJANGO
(Lee Perry)
UPSETTERS
Produced by:
Lee Perry
℗ 1969

HIGH Note
DISTRIBUTED BY
TIP TOP RECORD
CENTRE
Unauthorised
Copying is
Prohibited
37 ORANGE ST.
KINGSTON
JAMAICA, W.I.
Vocal
45 R.P.M.
S. 11
EVERYBODY NEEDS LOVE
BY
SLIM SMITH

85

Chapter 10 Labrish[1]

As far as I know me and Scratch still supposed to be alright but what Scratch do now... when he bring on this it was to get people off of him. So Scratch is my friend but he might tell you different 'cause we have a few things that we don't see eye to eye on... but there's plenty things you have to put in this book. Like it was me who cause Scratch to come to England and get him a car from Pama... the purple Jaguar!

Labrish is a thing when you tease people, you know. In Jamaica it means you tell stories about each other... jokes you know? Like a comedy thing. We were at Tubbys one night and Tubbys a solder[2] and me and Scratch were in a jovial mood and we went and said *"make we just talk over some rhythm"*. Tubbys catch our levels, you know, 'pon this dub thing and we just started to talk something on it. It became a serious joke. Me and Scratch just go in the studio and we start talk about some labrish.

---

[1] Labrish: idle talk, gossip, to bear tales
And also the title of a bizarre 1973 seven inch record credited to The Upsetters and Agrovators where Bunny Lee (as Pharaoh) and Lee Perry (as Moses) bemoan the current political situation, their own financial status, the state of the music business and ridicule other prominent record producers of the time. The pair mock Rupie Edwards for disappearing from the scene and deride Winston 'Niney' Holness for dressing like a business man and for paying artist royalties. Clancy Eccles comes in for some inspired invective for his support of the People's National Party. Clancy was a key organiser for the PNP Bandwagon during the election campaign of 1971/1972 when many artists and producers had supported the PNP. Striker recalled: *"In 1971 when Michael Manley was campaigning the PNP used my tune 'Better Must Come' by Delroy Wilson* (Justice (Jamaica)/Jackpot JP 763 (UK) 7") *and Maxie Romeo's 'Let The Power Fall For I'* ('Let The Power Fall For I' – Max Romeo - Hop (Jamaica)/Pama Supreme PS 306 (UK) 7"... *but Derrick Morgan did produce that... and the music reached the people and won the election. The music would speak for itself with all the artists of the time on the Bandwagon."* In March 1972 the PNP came to power in Jamaica and Striker and Scratch claim that Clancy can no longer afford to drive a car. The other side of the original release, 'Power Pressure' by Cornell Campbell, is a plea to Joshua (Michael Manley) to *"take the rod from off our back"* and further indication of a general undercurrent of dissatisfaction with the PNP government
[2] Tubbys a solder: King Tubby also repaired amplifiers and domestic appliances

Labrish

Labrish – The Upsetters & The Agrovators – Attack 7" (Jamaica) 1973

Wha' happen[1] Pharaoh? Gi' I a cigarette now

Boy, Brother Moses, the heart is willing but the pocket is weak
The power man and the rod man[2] them raise everything. I can't afford it

What?

Hail Pharaoh…

Love Brother Moses…

Man. What a gwaan?[3]

Man. The heat is on

You can say that again
Then how business a go?

Can't be worse, Brother Moses
I good fe bankrupt any moment now

What? So you can't get a loan?

What? Any bank you check now all you can hear is the bank manager a
moan and the tellers them a groan 'cause them a get hold up

What?

A true Sir

---

[1] wha' happen?: greeting: what's happening?
[2] the power man and the rod man: People's National Party; rod man from PNP leader Michael
Manley's Rod of Correction and power man from Manley's election pledge to give *power to the
people* as in Max Romeo's 'Let The Power Fall For I'
[3] what a gwaan: greeting: what's going on?

Man. They look like them killing us softly

Yes. Me can't connect that at all

Every day you return a bounced cheque

Ya so?

Man it dread
Nothing can't beat we now
Can't get nothing fe eat. We a suffer

So a judgement on the land Dread?

Yes Sir. A revelation time
Yes!
So how you feed the pickney them[1] a yard?[2]

Only God can tell you that Brother Moses. I don't even know
I don't even know how I exist myself. Can't get no dunny[3] Sir

So it kinda funny?

Yes Sir

Fire?

Yes. Revelation time Brother Moses

On the wire?

Yes Sir

---

[1] pickney them: pickney is a child, especially a very young child, (from pickaninny). Adding 'them' after a word in patois makes the plural so 'pickney them' are children
[2] yard: home
[3] dunny: money

Labrish

So long time I no see all I spar Jah Rupie[1]. Wonder what happened to him?

I hear him gone to the hills and the pressure is on

What happened to Brother Clancy?[2]

Power give him a beating. Yes...
Gi' you a little joke about Brother Clancy
When the other party did in power him there (did) a drive
But fe him party in power now all of them a walk

How?

A the rod a beat him!

Yes. Brother Clancy a get a beating
Right now him a mascot[3]

Power in session?
Yes

Ahhh... ohhh...
Can't connect

Them him friend Niney[4] too. Me have one labrish to give you about him
Him no stop wear suit and necktie too
Him gone like him an idiot too

I think it's because he pay the twelve and half cent royalty you know

A the power... the power skank!

A the power and the poor artists...

---

[1] Jah Rupie: Rupie Edwards: singer, record shop proprietor and record producer
[2] Brother Clancy: Clancy Eccles
[3] mascot: a fool, a person of no consequence
[4] Niney: Winston 'Niney The Observer' Holness

We call Scratch the Clown Prince Of Reggae! Not the Crown Prince... the Crown Prince is Dennis Brown... but Scratch is the Clown Prince. Scratch just have this thing with his artists like *"Don't come check me! Go check Trojan for your royalties! I can't talk to you now!"* but that's just Scratch. He has this big gyow[1] thing with his artists... it works for him!

Like when he's there 'pon the stage and he says *"Do you want to know Jesus?"* If he was not behaving like a man of unsound mind now they would arrest him![2] What him can get away with! They say he's a joker and he's a mad genius but if Scratch stopped it all now no-one would go and see him! His shows and everything would be a flop. So he has to continue doing what he's doing. You understand? It's coming like a friend of mine named Scully... that's Zoot Simms who used to sing with Alton Ellis... Alton used to say that when Scully lied even Scully believed the lie! So Scratch started believing in the madness and the things what him do... but Scratch will sit down with you and do things a madman can't do like go 'pon his lap top!

Scratch is what you call a ginal[3] or a gyower[4]. You know what a gyower is in Jamaica? A smart man. In England they'd say Scratch is a clever man. Right? That's his way... his eccentric way. It's like Howard Hughes[5] used to do fe him things. They didn't say Howard Hughes was a madman. They said he was a genius. He stayed behind the scenes for years and directed a multi-million dollar business. He carried them go a court and win... you remember?

So... that's Scratch. Every man does his thing a little way different... but him is a great producer.

---

[1] gyow: false/untrue
[2] Striker is referring to Scratch's alleged lewd behaviour at the Essential Music Festival, Brighton, UK in May 1996
[3] ginal: ginal/jinal: a clever person especially a crafty, tricky person
[4] gyower: liar
[5] Howard Hughes: Born 24th December 1905. Died 5th April 1976. Once one of the richest men in the world the American aviator, engineer, philanthropist, film producer and director was infamous for his eccentric behaviour and reclusive lifestyle

Bunny 'Striker' Lee, Toronto

COXSONE RECORDS

JAMAICA MUSIC   PUBLISHERS

I Am Still Waiting
The Wailers

MFG. BY JAMAICA RECORD MFG. CO. LTD., 13 BRENTFORD RD., KGN 5, JA., W.I.

ISLAND RECORDS LTD., 108, CAMBRIDGE ROAD, LONDON. N.W.6.

IT'S REGGAE TIME

Island Music

island RECORDS

45 R.P.M.

BZX-26.
WI-316
(A)

D. TONY LEE
Produced by: B. Lee
℗ 1968

SHO-BE-DO-BE DO (I LOVE YOU)
(Alton Ellis. Stanley Pemberton)

AMS 7093-A
℗ 1973
ADVANCE PROMOTION

AMS 7093
COPY
Side 1
2.59

A&M RECORDS

45 r.p.m.

WORKHOUSE

NOT FOR SALE
RELEASE DATE:
15—11—73

ALTON ELLIS
Produced by David Hadfield
REVOLUTION/RONDOR
MUSIC

Duke Reid

* DUKE REID PRESENT *

GREATEST HITS

D.R. Enterpr
B.M.I.
33 Bond Street
Kingston, Ja.
Tel: 25629
27594

THE TIDE IS HIGH
THE PARAGONS

RECORDED AT TREASURE ISLE RECORDING STUDIO

HARRY J.'s

Harry J. Record
Kingston, Ja.

45 R.P.M.

YOUNG, GIFTED AND BLACK
(Simone - Irvine)
BOB & MARCIA

TROJAN RECORDS

London Tree
Music Ltd.
℗ 1970

TR-7750 A

LOVE OF THE COMMON PEOPLE
(J. Hurley/R. Wilkins)
NICKY THOMAS
Produced by: Joel Gibson
Arranged and conducted by:
Johnny Arthy

Chapter 11 Reggae Hit The Town

Every era the words change and come with a different style...like a man used to say how reggae came in... *"See that streggae there?"* but the radio station wouldn't play it so we had to change the name to reggae! A ragamuffin was a thief and a robber. Men would say *"Don't bring that ragamuffin in a me yard. You keep company with too much ragamuffin..."* and now it's a big thing but most of the English people don't understand that ragamuffin was a thief... a pickpocket.

Do you know what reggae really is? Reggae[1] is the same as rock steady but with the organ shuffle. It's the shuffle that kind a carried up the rock steady... if you take out that you get rock steady! The organ shuffle kind a make it sound a little faster... the shuffling... plenty people a talk but they don't know. Reggae is the organ shuffle... I hear a whole heap of man say they brought in reggae and all of that but it's a lie them a tell 'cause we did it in 1968 in Duke Reid's studio.

Rock steady never had the organ shuffle. On a rock steady tune a horn man just played an intro, a solo and a little fill in. 'Bangarang'[2] was the first reggae tune... it had the shuffle right through. It was a foreign tune. A jazz tune named 'Bongo Chant'[3] but the guys were young as musicians and they couldn't hold

---

[1] 'It's Reggae Time' – D. Tony Lee – WIRL (Jamaica)/Island W1 3160 (UK) 7" 1968 released towards the end of the year and one of the first records to use reggae in it's title. D. Tony Lee is Striker's brother Don... also known as 'Stagger' Lee

[2] 'Bangarang' – Lester Sterling & Stranger Cole –
Carifta & Lee's (Jamaica)/Unity UN 502 (UK) 7" 1968

[3] 'Bongo Chant' - Kenny Graham & His Afro Cubists – Starlite ST45 013 (UK) 7" 1960

the chords to the bridge. So I said to Lester Sterling *"make it into a two chord tune"* and *"bam am bam... bam bad a day"* in the bridge and Lester just came back and played his own melody. We said we can't use the words and Stranger Cole and Lloyd Charmers were there and Lester said *"How 'Bangarang' sound to you?"* and I said *"Make we try it now... (sings) Woman no want bangarang"*. It's just a take off from 'Bongo Chant'. It kinda come like an original tune added to the other part of Kenny's tune so it ended up different. When it came out on the road it was the biggest tune for 1968 in Jamaica.

I did some rock steady tunes with Derrick Morgan and they came out and never hit... never went on with anything. I said *"Well, rahtid* [1] *... people them like this sound you know Glen* [2]. *I want you to dub the reggae in a the 'Seven Letters'"* [3]. So I dubbed in the reggae organ and I sent it to Pama and Trojan to put it out... the two companies... and it still go in the British charts. Pama and Trojan put 'Seven Letters' [4] out with Derrick Morgan with the *"schf, schf"* shuffling on the organ and it was a big hit on the British chart! That is the reggae! The organ a go *"reggae, reggae, reggae"*. That is the real reggae! When a man talks about reggae they don't really know what they talking about if they don't talk about the organ shuffle [5] but it's an important thing in the music. It bring back Derrick Morgan right on top but when it came out first nothing ever happened with the tune. When we dubbed in the reggae it was something different.

Every tune we did Coxsone used to have a cut to it. He'd always do it over... that's why me and him have the same set of tunes because I started doing what he did! He did over 'Bangarang' and released it up here in London first [6]. Like 'The Whip' with Owen Gray [7]... so when it came out the other day [8] everyone

---

[1] rahtid: exclamation indicating annoyance or amazement
[2] Glen: Glen Adams
[3] 'Seven Letters' – Derrick Morgan – Carib-Disc-Co (Jamaica) 1969
[4] 'Seven Letters' – Derrick Morgan - Crab CR 08 (UK) 7" (Pama) 1969
& 'Seven Letters' – Derrick Morgan - Jackpot JP 700 (UK) 7" (Trojan) 1969
[5] *"I'd started to record before I started in a band... I used to get sessions and Bunny Lee was the first producer I ever worked for but I used to play a couple of tunes for Mrs Pottinger too. I used to play the piano or the organ but whenever I played with 'Snapping'* (Theophilus 'Easy Snapping' Beckford) *it was the organ. 'Snapping' was not an organ man. Strictly a piano man! When I played with a next musician I'd play piano... Bunny Lee always used to love the organ shuffle."*
Ossie Hibbert
[6] 'Bangarang' - The Soul Vendors: 'Swing Easy' – Various Artists
– Coxsone CSL 8018 (UK) LP 1968
[7] 'The Whip' – The Soul Vendors: 'Soul Vendors On Tour' – Various Artists – Coxsone CSL 8010 (UK) LP & 'Blue Beat Special' – Various Artists - Coxsone CSP 1 (UK) LP 1968
[8] 'The Whip': Striker is referring to another recent re-release of this perennially popular record on the UK revival circuit

thought it was Coxsone's. But you know it was Mrs Pottinger who did the original one with the Ethiopians[1]. Every tune that hit in Jamaica...

And the people who published 'Bangarang' fight about the publishing. I don't know if Kenny Graham is still alive but you have to say it's his tune... all that happened is the bridge is different and the words. The words were changed to a Jamaican word (sings) *"Woman no want bangarang..."* Bangarang is a Jamaican word that means like *"Boy he's come here to make trouble, you know, come here to make pure bangarang"*[2]. If they say the man cause too much bangarang that means he is a trouble maker... they even used it in the House of Representatives when the opposition leader said *"It's going to be a bangarang!"* They changed it (sings) *"Jamaica no want no bangarang..."* so it kind a shifted from that because everything he said is going to be a bangarang. It's like when they say it's going to be *"hell and powder house"*[3]. That means it's war!

But in 'Bangarang'... if you listen Stranger Cole says something down towards the end and Lloyd Charmers says something different. I just said *"Make it go on..."* One of Roland Alphonso's biggest tunes was the version to 'Everybody Needs Love'[4] and we did it in Coxsone's studio[5]... '1,000 Tons Of Megaton'[6]. Roland played alto sax and Derrick Morgan deejayed 'pon it. If you listen to it you can hear Derrick make a mistake... Sylvan Morris[7] wanted to stop the tape. *"Cool it man!"* and I said *"No. Make it stay..."* he was doing it the same time as Roland was blowing and Family Man was playing one of Coxsone's organs. If you stopped everybody had to stop in those days! Then everybody would have to start over... sometimes an error would be made in a tune and you'd say *"Just make it ride. Take this man! Nobody will ever notice it..."* I have plenty of tunes where one singer would say something and the other would say something else.

When Derrick Morgan did talk on the record he made a mistake in it one time towards the end. Sylvan Morris was going to stop but I said *"Morris make it run with the mistake..."* If you listen his tongue gets tied up *"As the farmer said to the potato I'll plant you today then... dig you tomorrow"*. But Roland was

---

[1] 'The Whip' – The Ethiopians – Gay Feet (Jamaica)/Doctor Bird DB 1096 (UK) 7" 1967
[2] bangarang: a great noise or disturbance among people; quarrelling
[3] *"hell and powder house"*: a great noise or disturbance among people; quarrelling
[4] 'Everybody Needs Love' – Slim Smith – High Note (Jamaica)/Unity UN 504 (UK) 7" 1969
[5] Studio One, 13 Brentford Road, Kingston 5, Jamaica
[6] '1,000 Tons Of Megaton' - Roland Alphonso with The Bunny Lee All Stars
– Unity (Jamaica)/Gas GAS 112 (UK) 7" 1969
"Here comes Roly Soul with one thousand tons of megaton..."
[7] Sylvan Morris: recording engineer at Studio One and Harry J

cooking and you could feel the horns so we just made it go on and put it out same way. When it came out it was a runaway hit and Roland couldn't believe that the record had his name on it... himself as a solo artist. Me and him do quite a lot of songs... and Tommy McCook later. Me and every one of them get on. Well you have 'Deadly' Hedley[1] he's still alive now. Val Bennett was the man that played 'Al Capone's Guns Don't Argue'.[2] 'Return of Django'[3] that's Val Bennett but them guys didn't get a chance... they didn't get paid but me and them used to be about them times and they came aboard with me. They helped me a lot as a young producer. They'd arrange the horn section and all that and when I sold a tune and get any money I'd split it with the crew. We'd go on the road and sell records and I'd say *"Val here's some money for the kids them but leave me with some money to go back and press... and so on"*.

---

[1] 'Deadly' Hedley: Felix 'Deadly Hedley' Bennett: saxophone
[2] 'Al Capone' - Prince Buster's All Stars
– Prince Buster Voice Of The People (Jamaica)/Blue Beat BB 324 (UK) 7" 1965
[3] 'Return of Django' – The Upsetters – Upsetter (Jamaica & UK US 301) 7" 1969

Yu Can Reggay ? Leandro 1969

LEE'S

10 East Ave.,
Kingston 13

HOLD YOU JACK
(Derrick Morgan)
DERRICK MORGAN
With Bunny Lee's All Stars

JAGUAR

J—14

Produced by:
B. Lee
Engineer:
Syd Bucknor

RIPE CHERRY
(Eric Donaldson)
DENNIS ALCAPONE
MANUFACTURED BY DYNAMIC SOUNDS, 15 BELL RD., KGN, JA.

sun shot

PRODUCED BY
PHIL PRAT

MY HEART IS GONE
(Ken Boothe)
JOHN HOLT

ALL RIGHTS OF THE OWNER OF THIS RECORD ARE RESERVED. ANY UNAUTHORISED COPYING IS PROHIBITED.

Jontom

PHONE 24285

15 MARK LANE
KINGSTON

THE ONE I LOVE
KEN BOOTH
With The Supersonics Band
MANUFACTURED BY WEST INDIES RECORDS LTD., JAMAICA, W.I.

Lion

Produced by:
Lloyd Chalmers

Ⓟ 1973
DYNAMIC
SOUNDS

L 25

SHEILA
MUSIC

WHAT A FESTIVAL
(Donaldson — Chalmers)
ERIC DONALDSON

UNAUTHORISED PUBLIC PERFORMANCE, BROADCASTING AND COPYING OF THIS RECORD PROHIBITED • MANUFACTURED BY DYNAMIC SOUNDS, 15 BELL RD., KGN., JA.

SCOTTY

Donald's
Record Mart
Phone: 26506

30 Maxfield
Ave.,
Vocal

PENNY FOR YOUR SOUND
(V. Smikle)
THE FEDERALS
GEORGE TUCKER
& HIS ORCHESTRA

98

Chapter 12 A Record By Max Romeo

My first labels were Lee then Lee's and a bad label named Unity with a black hand and a white hand shaking hands over a mountain that tore down the place with Pama. A guy named Smokey Joe gave me the idea for the label and it brought the biggest set of hits. 'Wet Dream'[1] and all those tunes there... 'Wet Dream' was a tune now!

ET[2] used to work at Coxsone's too you know and the first tune he ever recorded was 'Wet Dream'. That's just come to show you! This is a serious joke! I wrote it after we were working in a studio on the Edgware Road in London... Pye or one of those studios there... I heard some guy in the cutting room say *"Boy me have a wet dream last night"* and the guys all ran jokes with the men there so I just wrote the tune about *"crumpet"* with *"wet dream"* and *"lie down gal make me push it up..."* and all that, you know, the English words. I put it on the 'Hold You Jack'[3] rhythm. 'Hold You Jack' was done at Duke Reid's studio. It was Derrick Morgan's rhythm and he'd sung a different tune 'pon the rhythm and I said to Derrick *"I want you to sing 'Wet Dream'"* but Derrick said *"No. I want to sing this tune called 'I Love You Down To My Liver'* or something like that 'pon it. I asked Pat Kelly and all those man to voice it and they said *"No. We nah go voice that slack tune..."* All the big names at the time... nobody wanted to sing it and Maxie[4] was the last man now.

---

[1] 'Wet Dream' Max Romeo – Unity UN 503 (UK) 7" 1969 A Number Ten UK hit
[2] ET: Errol 'ET' Thompson. Born 29th December 1948. Died 13th November 2004. Jamaica's foremost recording engineer
[3] 'Hold You Jack' – Derrick Morgan – Lee's (Jamaica)/Island WI 3159 (UK) 7" 1968
[4] Maxie: Max 'Romeo' Smith

Maxie used to sing for Ken Lack in a group named The Emotions but at that time he wasn't singing. He was a good singer but he had concentrated more on selling records after Ken Lack had left the business and he was working for me as a salesman. So I turned to Maxie and I said *"Everyday you want to voice a tune... even on a flipside... so as you can play it to your girlfriend"*. He said *"Boy Striker I don't want to sing it"* and I said *"If you don't sing this tune then don't come to work tomorrow!"*

So I said *"Come Maxie... make we go inna the studio"* and we voiced it up at Coxsone's studio. Coxsone had gone out to the bathroom to wash his face and I said to ET *"you take the tune"*. Glen said to Maxie *"Come round here and do this! One cut!"* and Maxie started (sings) *"Every night me go to sleep me have wet dream..."* and as the tune finished Glen Adams shouted *"In deh!"* and Coxsone said *"No!"* He came back and raised Cain! *"No Jack! You have to just wipe off that because you can't do those kind of tunes in my studio... I don't want that tune recorded here!"* and I said *"No Beat[1]... you can't wipe it off"* but he said the session had to stop. That's the only time me and Coxsone have any hard talking! Anyway we got the tune mixed and sent it up to England to Mr Palmer... used it as a tune to make up the numbers with Pama... a flip side or a b side or something.

Next thing Harry Palmer called me one day and said that me and Maxie Romeo have to come to England. *"Bunny I want Maxie to do shows 'cause the tune a start to mash up England"* but in those days Maxie never had a passport. Max Smith was his right name and you can imagine how quick we made up a passport for Maxie. The record spent twenty six weeks in the British chart[2] and any time after that if I told a singer what to do then they had to do it! Maxie was the first one out of them all to come 'pon tour in England.

All the big singers... Pat Kelly... Slim Smith... started that they'd never done shows in England! Maxie was the first man out of the whole clan to come. The least of the apostles... the underdog... was the first man to go in the British

---

[1] Beat: Clement 'Coxsone' Dodd was known as Downbeat or Beat
[2] 'Wet Dream' spent twenty five weeks in the British Charts in 1969 *"coming like Frank Sinatra and 'My Way' "* with no radio play: the BBC banned it and Alan Freeman used to describe it as *"a record by Max Romeo"* on the Sunday afternoon weekly chart run down on Radio One. Mecca Ballrooms also banned the record. Max attempted to explain to the UK music press that the song was not rude at all but referred to his leaking roof: he was asking his girlfriend to move out of the way as he tried to push a broom up into the hole to stop said leak *"Lie down girl let me push it up, push it up. Lie down..."*

charts. A big thing! From 'Wet Dream' you don't know what's going to hit... so after that if I told a man to sing a tune... even if it was foolishness... he would do it. You understand?

Max Romeo

DUPPY CONQUEROR
(B. Marley — L. Perry)
BOB MARLEY & THE WAILERS

MR. BROWN
(B. Marley — L. Perry)
BOB MARLEY & THE WAILERS

Produced by:
P. Weston

Dist.
Micron Music Ltd.
14 Retirement Rd.,
Kingston 5.

STRAIGHT TO JAZZBO'S HEAD
(I. Roy)
I. ROY

NO WOMAN, NO CRY
(Bob Marley)
Produced by STEVE SMITH & CHRIS BLACKWELL
Live at the Lyceum, London

Time: 3.57

BOB
MARLEY
and THE
WAILERS

WIP 6244-A
WIPX 1426

Rondor Music
London Ltd

℗ 1974 Island
Records Ltd

BARON'S

Dist. By
THE
BARON'S
RECORD
CENTER

94 Molynes
Rd., Kgn. 10
Prod. By
B. SMITH

MOSQUITO 1
EL PASSO
With Tommy McCook &
The Supersonics

WILD FLOWER

Made in Jamaica   ® Regd. Trade Mark

326 A
XYZ PROD.

Engineer:
G. Raymond
Producer:
L. Charmers

EVERYTHING I OWN
(D. GATES)
KEN BOOTHE

103

Chapter 13 Vocal Version... The Singers

A man like me now... I have known a lot of great singers. When you're hot you're hot and that's the time you should a strike. Strike the iron when it's hot. Every one of them was good in their own right.

Johnny Clarke hit with the flying cymbals and then Cornell Campbell hit too! Those two ruled the roost for a long time. Johnny Clarke is still one of the greatest. Johnny Clarke's common law wife was my sister Audrey and she has three children for him. He's the only singer to give Dennis Brown[1] trouble during his reign and Dennis did sing a tune: *"Your boasting can only be for a time"*.[2]

 How I used to do it... if you're swinging then you're the one carrying back the bacon and the bread. You're all in this stable and the others have to get the money too... because one day the day will come when you're going to get money off of them. Just treat everybody as a family because the moment you ever favourise this man over that man it will never work. Of course you can tell a man *"I don't like this or I don't like that"* but keep it steady. Every man is a man and every man is a star in his own right and their day will come. Look how long Beres Hammond a sing before him come 'pon the headlines!

But Slim Smith was like a favourite. Slim Smith was very good friend of mine... him have a good personality. I met Slim Smith when Derrick Morgan and myself went to a stage show... that was the first time I heard Slim Smith with

---

[1] Dennis Emanuel Brown: Born 1st February 1957. Died 1st July 1999
[2] 'Boasting' – Dennis Brown – 'Wolf & Leopards' – DEB Music (Jamaica & UK) LP 1976

The Techniques and I said *"Derrick that guy sound like Clyde McPhatter*[1]. I have to go and meet him 'cause I like how he sings". So after the stage show we went round and I was introduced to Slim and, from that time, me and him were friends right on. Slim is an incomparable singer even though he's been dead thirty odd, coming on for forty, years. Slim was the nearest thing to Curtis Mayfield[2] and he could also play instruments... look how long Slim Smith dead and you hear his music still.

Do you know of another singer who's come up like Slim Smith? Some men like Dave Barker[3], Cornell Campbell and probably Ken Parker sound near to him but you've never had another singer who's made that impact on Jamaican music like Slim Smith. Not even Bob Marley... The Paragons[4] ... any time Slim Smith and The Uniques would sing Slim used to beat them up! Not physically you understand!

Slim started out with The Techniques and Winston Riley... a guy name Franklyn and one named Frederick that was the father of one of Musical Youth[5]... you know? Slim Smith was Keith Smith. Coxsone named him Slim through he was a slim person... gave him the nickname and just called him Slim Smith. He did a stint with Coxsone after he left The Techniques... he and I went up to Coxsone and Slim did some tunes with him. Slim did quite a lot of tunes with Coxsone and some of them have never been released all now... this was before I started recording for myself. When we were voicing 'Everybody Needs Love' I did the rhythm at Duke Reid's and carried it to Coxsone to voice it to get that combination. Coxsone was engineering himself and before Slim did start singing he said to me *"Jackson... why waste your time? You no see a*

---

[1] Clyde McPhatter: Born 15th November 1932. Died 13th June 1972. Distinguished American rhythm & blues and soul vocalist. Original lead singer with Billy Ward & The Dominoes and The Drifters

[2] Curtis Mayfield: Born 3rd June 1942. Died 26th December 1999. American rhythm & blues and soul singer and songwriter, lead singer with The Impressions, and a major influence on the development of Jamaican music. *"The godfather of reggae"* David Rodigan

[3] Dave Barker: one of Jamaica's best, but still seriously under rated, singers and deejays. As one half of Dave & Ansel Collins he topped the UK National Charts with 'Double Barrel' (Techniques TE 901) in spring 1971. Their follow up release 'Monkey Spanner' (Techniques TE 914) reached Number Seven in the summer of that year

[4] The Paragons: peerless Jamaican vocal group that included Garth 'Tyrone' Evans, Bob Andy, Junior Menz, and Leroy Stamp. In 1964 Stamp was replaced by John Holt and Howard Barrett replaced Junior Menz. One of their biggest hits 'The Tide Is High' – Trojan & Duke Reid Greatest Hits (Jamaica)/Treasure Isle TI 7009 (UK) 7" from 1967 has become a pop standard covered by Blondie in 1980 (a UK & USA Number One hit) and Atomic Kitten in 2002 (a UK Number One hit)

[5] Musical Youth: Frederick Waite formed Musical Youth in the UK with two of his sons Junior and Patrick *"Frederick Waite used to play guitar and he still does now with Musical Youth"* taking them to worldwide success with their 'Full Up' – Sound Dimension (Studio One (Jamaica) 7" 1968/'Pass The Kouchie' (Mighty Diamonds – Music Works (Jamaica) 7" 1981) update entitled 'Pass The Dutchie' (MCA YOU 1 7") in 1982. It went on to sell over four million copies

singer's done when I done with him?" so I said to Slim *"Just sing round the mixing board"* and Slim blew him away! That was 'Everybody Needs Love' and that was Slim Smith's biggest hit up to date. It was awesome, man. Coxsone was round the board and he couldn't move! Slim really sing him away. 'Everybody Needs Love' and then we did a version with Roland Alphonso... it was his biggest tune too! 'One Thousand Tons Of Megaton'.

When I formed The Uniques it was with a tune named 'People Get Ready To Do Rock Steady'[1]... that was the first tune I recorded with Slim Smith. Ken Boothe and Derrick Morgan sang the harmony. You'd have to say they were the first Uniques. Lloyd Charmers came in when we did 'Let Me Go Girl'. Then Charmers brought in his brethren Jimmy Riley. You understand? Through Slim used to sing lead with The Techniques I came up with the name The Uniques. Them days you'd have to think!

It was Slim taught Dennis Brown to play guitar when they were living in two big yards. Slim lived on Orange Street on the corner behind Coxsone's Record Shop and Dennis lived in the big yard on North Street. Dennis Brown used to call Delroy Wilson The Teacher and that's why Dennis Brown was so versatile because Slim Smith and Delroy Wilson taught him. Delroy Wilson and Slim Smith... great artists. Two of the greatest artists... it's them did bring and teach Dennis Brown. All those singers used to like to listen to one another... anytime you'd voice Slim Smith or Delroy Wilson then you'd find Alton Ellis[2] up at the studio listening to them.

Alton Ellis was a great artist too... Alton was alright. I have enough material with Alton to do an LP... me and Alton do a lot of work but not like me and John Holt! Alton used to come to England a lot. The police did take Alton's car once and I said to Alton *"Just come down the station with me and we'll tell the man we've come for Alton's car!"* They said *"There's your car man. It's alright"*. Alton was a good man. He's a singer who takes a little longer because he's a professional... a perfectionist right?

Alton used to be a senior man at Duke Reid and then he went on tour with Coxsone[3]. Duke was really vexed when he went with Coxsone you know. Duke never forgave Alton for that... never forgave him. He'd said to Alton *"Don't go and I'll send you up with The Supersonics"*. He believed in Alton Ellis 'cause you see when Alton left Duke he started working with The Paragons and Duke

---

[1] 'People Rock Steady' – The Uniques – Lee's (Jamaica)/Island WI 3070 (UK) 7" 1967
[2] Alton Nehemiah Ellis: Born 1st February 1938. Died 11th October 2008
[3] Soul Vendors 1967 UK Tour featuring vocalists Ken Boothe & Alton Ellis

Reid had the power to make a man hits! Duke's biggest set of hits were with Alton in the old days and he treated Alton as a son. But Coxsone was smart man and he persuaded Alton to come to England and when Alton went over to Coxsone they did over all of Duke's tunes. But that mashed up Coxsone's thing too because he took over Delroy Wilson's position and Delroy and the rest of Coxsone's artists got vexed. Then Coxsone went on like he never wanted to carry Alton you know. Ken Boothe will give you that story! He said *"No, man!"* and Alton had come with his suitcase and his visa... but Coxsone was a different man. Him alright though.

Alton Ellis and his sister Hortense![1] She was one of the greatest woman singers... she don't get recognition yet but some time to come she's going to get it. No other woman could sing like that girl. She was brilliant man! She could sing anything! Anything she sing with Jackie Edwards, Derrick Morgan or her brother... she was just brilliant. You understand?

You know how Alton did get to live in England? Him and Slim Smith did a tune for a guy named Stanley Pembleton who worked for A&M Records[2] but after Slim died Stanley asked me *"Who else can take Slim's place?"* and the first one that came to mind was Cornell Campbell but he didn't have a passport. So I said what about Ken Parker? He said *"Can Ken Parker fit the bill?"* and I said *"Yes!"* so he sent for Alton[3] and Ken Parker[4]. Then Ken was living here for a little while too... we need to talk about Ken Parker as he's a great artist too. He has a Sam Cooke[5] sound. He was living up here but he left and went back to Jamaica... he's in Miami now. Ken Parker is a very good artist. He put out a lot of hits for Joe Gibbs, Duke Reid and myself.

Delroy Wilson had a tune named 'I'm Still Waiting' for Federal... Lloyd Charmers did produce it for Federal... and the people in England them wanted it but they couldn't get it[6] so I just went back to Jamaica and make it over with

---

[1] Hortense Mahalia Ellis: Born 18th April 1941. Died 18th October 2000

[2] *"I was in England hoping to be closer to the big recording studios..."* Alton Ellis

[3] 'Sho Be Do Be Do (I Love You)' – Alton Ellis - A&M (Jamaica) & 'Sho Be Do Be Do (I Love You)'/'I Love You True' – Alton Ellis A&M (Jamaica & AMS 7093 UK) 7" 1973

[4] 'We Must Be In Love' – Slim Smith/'I Wish I Could Make You Mine' – Alton Ellis - A&M AMS 7092 (UK) 7" 1973. Both sides are credited to Ken Parker on the UK release

[5] Sam Cooke: Samuel 'Sam' Cooke: Born 22nd January 1931. Died 11th December 1964. Inspirational American gospel, soul and pop singer

[6] 'I'm Still Waiting' – Delroy Wilson – LTD (Jamaica) 7" 1976. Delroy Wilson's interpretation of The Wailers' 'I Am Still Waiting' was one of his biggest ever hits. However, the record was not released outside of Jamaica at the time and was only available elsewhere in limited quantities in specialist record shops as an expensive import, or pre-release, single

Delroy one Sunday. The Monday it was out on the road and it mashed up the whole place! It killed the one that the Khouris, who ran Federal Records, had a hold on. That's why I know sometimes when a singer is hot or a tune is hot and you hold it then the singer's getting held up too. When he decides to do it over it kills the other one. Because I always say if I work with a singer and he goes outside and has a hit I have to have it for my records too. Unless me and the man move good and they say *"Bunny. You can get a cut for an LP for your purpose..."* but you can bet your life I'm going to make it over with the same singer! So I always call in back the singer and do it!

Pat Kelly, Slim Smith, Jackie Edwards[1], Owen Gray... everybody can sing. You name them. Pat Kelly's tune at the time was 'How Long'[2]... he made other hits but he never made a tune bigger than 'How Long'. The same with Slim Smith and 'Everybody Needs Love'[3] although everybody always talks about 'The Time Has Come'[4] it only hit after him dead! Jackie Edwards is another great. We call Jackie Edwards 'The Maestro'. Jackie used to say to me *"Bunny I'm going to make you rich one day... even if I'm dead! One day you're going to get rich off a Jackie Edwards"*. Me and Chris Blackwell always believed in him. Roy Shirley is a great artist too. We were brethren from before...

John Holt and myself go way back... I took John Holt to Canada and he didn't like it! I took him to England in 1970 when Junior Lincoln kept a big show[5]. John wasn't supposed to be on the show but he sang with The Cimarons[6]... they rehearsed in the dressing room! Nicky Thomas[7], The Maytals, Desmond Dekker and Bob & Marcia[8] were there. Coxsone and Byron Lee[9] were there too... quite a few producers from Jamaica.

U Roy also brought in this thing when they played a singer's tunes he'd say *"Johnny Clarke showcase"* and *"John Holt showcase"* on the mic. and I

---

[1] Wilfred Gerald 'Jackie' Edwards: Born1940. Died 9th August 1992. singer and songwriter

[2] 'How Long' – Pat Kelly – Pama (Jamaica)/ Gas GAS 115 (UK) 7" 1969

[3] 'Everybody Needs Love' – Slim Smith – High Note (Jamaica)/Unity UN 504 (UK) 7" 1969

[4] 'The Time Has Come' – Slim Smith – High Note (Jamaica)/Pama PM 850 (UK) 7" 1972

[5] The Caribbean Music Festival, Empire Pool, Wembley April, 1970

[6] The Cimarons: excellent UK based reggae group who often backed visiting Jamaican artists on live dates in addition to recording their own material

[7] Nicky Thomas: Cecil Nicholas 'Nicky' Thomas. Born 30th May 1949. Died 1990. Nicky's biggest hit was 'Love Of The Common People' (Joe Gibbs (Jamaica)/Trojan TR 7750 (UK) 7" a Number Nine UK hit in 1970

[8] Bob & Marcia: Bob Andy & Marcia Griffiths: two hugely talented Jamaican singers and songwriters enjoying crossover success at the time with 'Young Gifted And Black' – Harry J (Jamaica & HJ 6605 UK) 7" a Number Five UK hit in 1970

[9] Byron Lee: Born 27th June 1935. Died 4th November 2008. Bass, bandleader, record producer and proprietor of Dynamic Sounds

thought *"Bam!"* and I made an album named the 'John Holt Showcase'[1]. We put some mirrors around John Holt for the cover and they reflected back like a showcase and we did it disco style and joined the rhythm and the vocal together. That LP sold like a forty five over the Christmas.

You see Ronnie Davis? Ronnie Davis changed his name about five different times to Romey Pickett and Romey Tennors because he used to sing with The Tennors till Ronnie Davis did over a Bob Marley tune named 'Kaya'[2] and he started to make him name from that. But because he kept changing his name it come like just the other day people discovered him after he'd been singing for so many years. He came and toured England and everybody was saying *"Ronnie Davis, Ronnie Davis..."* and collectors started to bring out tunes with him now and say *"Did you sing this?"* You understand?

'Cherry Oh Baby'?[3] Heh, heh, heh... up to now they don't beat that one. It's the biggest hit in Jamaica and the Caribbean so far. I did that song about five times but the really big 'Cherry Oh Baby' was one Saturday morning. Well... one night the Festival eliminations were on and I went along with Delroy Wilson and some of the other artists. When this guy, Eric Donaldson, sung the tune Delroy bring him to me and I decided... whether it get picked or not... to record it the next day. At that time I was producing things for Dynamic. Sid Bucknor[4] was working with Eric Donaldson before this and because Sid was the engineer at Dynamics Eric didn't want to do it. So that morning I reached early and put Eric in a chair at Dynamics. Neville Lee[5] came in and said *"What's that ugly boy doing in my chair?"* and Tommy Cowan[6] said *"No, No, Neville! This guy a tear up the Festival thing last night! Him have a tune that a go mash up the place and Striker Lee did bring him come to record it!"* and they okayed the

---

[1] 'The John Holt Showcase (New Disco Style)'- John Holt – Thunderbolt (Jamaica) LP 1977
[2] 'Kaya' - Ronnie Davis – Attack (Jamaica)/Jamaica Sound JS 911 (UK) 7" 1978
[3] 'Cherry Oh Baby'/'Sir Charmers Special' – Eric Donaldson – Jaguar J 08 (Jamaica)/Dynamic DYN 420 (UK) 7" 1971. Tommy Cowan recalled *"From the moment I heard Eric at the rehearsals for the Festival Song entrants those present knew we were hearing the winner"*. Played in Bunny's new 'broken beat' style 'Cherry Oh Baby' established Eric Donaldson, former vocalist with The West Indians, as a major star. It was covered by both The Rolling Stones and UB 40 and was the inspiration behind a revival in the early Nineties that produced numerous updated digital versions of the rhythm. Eric Donaldson is a household name in Jamaica and will always be associated with the Festival Song Contest which he has won an incredible seven times. Acknowledged as Jamaica's biggest selling record ever it remains the most popular Festival song of all time and, every year, the judges complain that there are far too many 'Cherry Oh Baby' sound-alikes
[4] Sid Bucknor: Sidney 'Siddy' Bucknor Died 9th May 2010. Recording engineer
[5] Neville Lee: Byron Lee's brother, then managing director at Dynamic Sounds, Neville would later leave Dynamic to establish Sonic Sounds Record Manufacturing and Distribution
[6] Tommy Cowan: lead singer with The Jamaicans who also worked for Dynamic Sounds

session. We did it in a studio that Byron Lee fixed up for me and Charmers but they didn't like the sound. It had a different sound...

I went back in and brought in Denzil Laing[1] and the band that I used was an outside band with my drummer Lloyd Adams who we called 'Tin Leg'. That band was The Inner Circle[2] and later half of it became Third World[3]... Ian and Roger, the Lewis brothers, went to America and 'Touter'[4] used to play organ with The Aggrovators. Ibo Cooper and Cat Coore they went off with Third World so... Third World was a part of 'Cherry Oh Baby'. Lloyd Charmers did a version of it too[5]. You remember one of the first versions that came out the b side was called 'Sir Charmers Special'[6]. It was called 'Sir Charmers Special' not 'Straight To Charmers Head' because Lloyd Charmers was my friend and I never wanted it to look too bad... so we just called it 'Sir Charmers Special'.

But sometimes these singers now, if you don't understand, seven man[7] will have the same song. Sometimes the first one comes out then the other man puts his one out and you can't blame him because he's spent the money on making the record and he can't afford not to put it out. That was one of the main problems with the Jamaican music industry... so if you come as a man from England and you acquire my tune a man will change the name and sell you the same tune because Horace Andy or Slim Smith had sung it for him too. If they see a chance they're going to make back a money and put it in their pocket. If it named 'Did' he'd sell it to you as 'Don't' and years later you'll say *"I have this already..."* It name 'Did' over here and 'Don't' over there and sometimes it's the same artist and just the name changed!

You know who's a good producer and nobody talks about him either? Phil Pratt[8]. Phil Pratt goes back a long way... he was in the business before me and I used to plug his records on the radio station but he was a very quiet person and he'd stay in the background even until now. He's running a restaurant now[9]. Phil Pratt, a guy named Calneck and myself we go back a long time. The first

---

[1] Denzil 'Pops' Laing: percussion
[2] 'Ripe Cherry' – Dennis AlCapone – Jaguar J 14 (Jamaica)/Dynamic DYN 422 (UK) 7" 1971 the b side version 'Red Cherry' is credited to The Inner Circle
[3] Inner Circle & Third World: internationally successful crossover bands
[4] Bernard 'Touter' Harvey: keyboards
[5] 'What A Festival' – Eric Donaldson/'Version Festival' – Eric Donaldson & I Roy
– Lion L 25 (Jamaica)/Dragon DRA 1017 (UK) 7" 1973
[6] 'Sir Charmers Special'/'Cherry Oh Baby' – Eric Donaldson
– Jaguar J 08 (Jamaica)/Dynamic DYN 420 (UK) 7" 1971
[7] record producers
[8] Phil Pratt: George Phillips, also known as Phillip Choukoe, better known as Phil Pratt
[9] Scandal West Indian Takeaway, 152 Manor Park Road, Harlesden. London NW10

tune he made was 'Sir Pratt Special'[1] and some bad Ken Boothe tunes from that time: 'You Left The Water Running' and 'The One I Love'[2] and some Helmsley Morris tunes like 'Little Things'[3]. Phil Pratt is an artist too but he likes to stay in the background. Plenty of Pat Kelly's hits away from me like 'They Talk About Love'[4] it's Phil Pratt who made them: John Holt with 'My Heart Is Gone'[5] and 'Strange Things'[6]... Phil Pratt. I want to tell you he recorded Horace Andy before Coxsone[7]... we used to call Horace Andy Sleepy. I did a lot of work with Horace Andy... he's great. Phil Pratt and Horace Andy did over some tunes that Horace did for me and I didn't know as me and Phil Pratt were friends but in two different camps. I was driving down the road with Horace Andy and we saw Phil Pratt and Horace got flat in a the car and I said *"What are you hiding for?"* and he said *"Boy I don't want Pratt to see me"* so I stopped the car and I said *"Wha' happen Phil? Horace is hiding from you...so what him do?"* He said *"Well Agro... he used to call me Agro... I don't know"* but I found out later when I put out 'Money Money'[8] and Pratt said *"but he's done that tune for me"* but mine came out and it was a hit. You understand?

Sometimes... up to this day in Jamaica they call it conman or ginalship[9] and that's what's held back this reggae industry because everyone wants to use their brain. Up here you say this man is clever or this man is a con. They want to get rich overnight so they'd give you, me and everyone the same tune under a different name. If everybody bought a copy the tune could go to Number One but you're not going to push it. You just want to make back your money and so the tune just dies. Nobody's going to say *"this tune is selling well this week"* so they hold themselves back! This music could have gone plenty, plenty, plenty far and, as I said, I did a lot of different works and promotions before I started producing records.

We didn't talk about the great Dennis Brown! He was smart! We did a whole heap of work me and D Brown. He was a great human being too... Dennis Brown. Ken Boothe, Slim Smith, Delroy Wilson was one of the greatest... John Holt... I have the record now for the longest selling Number One in Jamaica with John Holt and 'Stick By Me'.

---

[1] 'Sir Pratt Special' – Vincent Gordon – Jontom (Jamaica)/Caltone TONE 104 (UK) 7" 1966
[2] 'The One I Love'/'You Left The Water Running'– Ken Boothe
 – Jontom (Jamaica)/Caltone TONE 106 (UK) 7" 1967
[3] 'Little Things – Helmsley Morris – Jontom Blank (Jamaica)/Jolly JY 007 (UK) 7" 1969
[4] 'They Talk About Love' – Pat Kelly – Sunshot (Jamaica)/Camel CA 65 (UK) 7" 1971
[5] 'My Heart Is Gone' – John Holt – Sunshot (Jamaica)/Smash SMA 2303 (UK) 7" 1970
[6] 'Strange Things' – John Holt – Sunshot (Jamaica)/Punch PH 60 (UK) 7" 1971
[7] 'Black Man's Country' - Horace Hinds – Jontom Blank (Jamaica) 7" 1966
[8] 'Money Money' – Horace Andy – Justice (Jamaica) 7" 1975
[9] ginalship: ginal/jinal: a clever person especially a crafty, tricky person so ginalship is dishonesty

And we didn't talk about Slim Smith as a person… but you see this business now once you have a favourite tune and a favourite singer you can never pass that. Say that you are a singer and I am your favourite singer then the other singers aren't going to stand a chance. No other singer gets a chance so you have to treat every singer as a man and every man as a man. Look on it like a wheel. If one spoke's out of line and you don't fix it then a next spoke's going to go till the whole wheel's mashed up. So even if you have a favourite singer or a favourite person in this business you can't show it and you have to treat every man as a man.

Alton Ellis

Pat Kelly

Jackie Edwards and Hortense Ellis

114

Chapter 14 Instrumental Version... The Musicians

Everything I do it's like I was a trendsetter...

Carlie and Family Man... those brothers were my rhythm section for a while. They started in the Sixties and people used to call them *"Bunny Lee and his wrong chord musicians"*. I used to say the people who buy records don't know chords like you do! But after we started making the hits everybody started using them and all the big musicians like Hux Brown then played with them. They called them the wrong chord musicians. *"They can play a dance out in the street but they don't know chords"* but they became the musicians of the day. They used to be the Bunny Lee All Stars but it never fair to the musicians.

My friend Larry Lawrence[1] used to tease Eddy Grant from The Equals[2] all the time and Eddy used to say *"Bunny, your friend is causing me agro"*. I said *"What is that Eddy?"* and he said *"aggravation"* meaning that he is annoying him. *"Talk to him, man"* because Larry always teased him. Up to now if I see Eddy Grant I call him Agro! *"Wha' happen Agro?"* and he says *"Yeah Bunny man!"* He's a good friend. So I said I liked the name and when I went back to Jamaica I'm going to call my group of guys The Aggrovators... that means they're going to give everybody trouble. That annoyed the other musicians...

---

[1] Larry Lawrence: Clifton 'Larry' Lawrence Born 1947. Died 25th August 2008. UK based Jamaican record producer and shop proprietor. Larry's shop moved from Kilburn High Road, London NW6 to Coldharbour Lane, Brixton, London SW9 in 1976. Larry's labels included Ethnic, Fight, Ethnic Fight & Larry's Records

[2] Eddy Grant: lead singer with The Equals who had a number of pop hits in the Sixties. Eddy later became a very successful solo artist

the big musicians! We couldn't afford the big guys like Jackie Jackson[1] and Winston Wright[2]... this was after Bobby Aitken stopped playing and said *"Me a go get a steady job now"*.

Then Scratch came with the name The Upsetters which was the same Aggrovators. Scratch couldn't afford the big musicians who played for Beverley's and Duke Reid either. Those guys had money so we couldn't cope with them! Our musicians tried their best to get good. And they got to sound good! The first tune that Family Man played with his brother Carlie was 'Watch This Sound'[3] with Slim Smith. They were a team together with Glen Adams who started playing the organ and Reggie playing guitar. The Upsetters and The Aggrovators with Family Man and Carlie... they became The Wailers band then Robbie[4] came in when they started to play for Bob. Robbie is a student of Family Man too you know. Joe Gibbs' Professionals were the same as The Aggrovators too... Reggie and Glen[5] and Family Man them. In the early days Joe Gibbs used to use Jackie Jackson and them but everybody got to know that my musicians got good and they started to use them. And, of course, they were cheaper so they came the same way...

And that's why I have some tunes that are classics up to this day... even though they said the chords were wrong when they played it back! But them nah go play the wrong chords! They just played it differently. Take a tune like 'Money, Money' that Horace Andy sang. The horns are out of tune right? And it bad! And look how many man licked over that rhythm but can't make it sound so! They even played the horns out of tune and they can't do it! You see what I'm talking about? I don't remember the year we made 'Money, Money' but I do know it's a classic. Yeah... you know everybody tried to make over that rhythm but they never got it right 'cause my horns were a little out of tune and the musicians didn't even know that. Barry Brown sings 'pon it too... a lot of singers sing 'pon it. I have a boss version of it... Brad from New York did put out this LP named 'King Of Dub'[6] and they slowed it down so you hear the bass come in (sings) *"Tood a doop. Tood a doop..."* You never hear that cut? That really is a bad album... 'King Of Dub'.

I have plenty of rhythms where the chords were wrong and mistakes were made and I'd say *"drop it out"* but the people like it! They were the hits! People love

---

[1] Jackie Jackson: Clifton 'Jackie' Jackson: bass
[2] Winston Wright: Winston 'Brubeck' Wright: organ
[3] 'Watch This Sound' – The Uniques – Tramp (Jamaica)/Trojan TR 619 (UK) 7" 1968
[4] Robert 'Robbie' Shakespeare: bass
[5] Glen: Glen Adams
[6] 'King Of Dub' – Clocktower (USA) LP 1979

it and the buying public don't know that. You understand? It's a mistake but the crowd them love it. We had a thing behind a tune one time and I didn't like it. This was a spur of the moment thing when we were mastering a tune named 'Jah Jah In There' by Johnny Clarke[1] but we'd pressed a couple so I went and mixed it back. But it's a good thing I did keep a copy of the record! I had to go master it back and put it back on the record again because the people wouldn't buy it! They wanted the spoiled version. I said to Miss P at Randy's *"If a man don't notice and him don't bring it back you sell off those! But this is the one you a go sell now"*.

I started to put the musicians' names on the LP sleeves because people never used to put on their names. I was the first to start that[2]. Give Caesar what him due![3] Who play organ. Who play what. And that's why these men made a name for themselves because now you could know Sly on drums or Santa on drums[4]. But me is a man who'd find them all lunch money and then carry them home. Sometimes my car had twenty men in it coming from Harry J's studio with some 'pon the top because I didn't leave anybody on the street. I even bought Robbie Shakespeare a bike! Then every musician got credit from the bank and every musician got credit for their car but some wouldn't pay and they left me holding the bag! I lost out 'cause it was me who had to pay as I was the guarantor.

Ansel Collins is a very versatile musician. See 'Double Barrel'[5] and all those things? Ansel Collins made those rhythms and sold them to Winston Riley. He was very creative. He made 'Night Doctor'[6] and Scratch got it to put out. He helped Sly on the drums too. I had a rhythm Tubbys called 'Flat Foot Hustling'[7]... a version to the 'Shank I Sheck' rhythm that Jackie Mittoo played

---

[1] 'Jah Jah In There': 'Enter His Gates With Praise' - Johnny Clarke
– Jackpot (Jamaica)/Lord Koos KOO 42 (UK) 7" 1974
[2] *"Bunny Lee was the first man to put musicians' names on an album… when Bunny start to do that everyone follow!"* Ossie Hibbert
[3] Give Caesar what him due!: 'Render therefore unto Caesar the things that are Caesar's'
The Gospel according to St Matthew Chapter 22, Verse 21 The Holy Bible
[4] 'Brass Rockers' - Bunny Lee & King Tubby Present Tommy McCook And The Aggravators – Total Sounds (Jamaica) LP 1975 features 'Introducing The Aggravators' on the back cover with superb studio photographs of Bernard 'Touter' Harvey: organ, Bobby 'Bobbie' Ellis: trumpet, Tony Chin: guitar, Ansel Collins: piano, Tommy McCook: tenor saxophone, Vin 'Trommie' Gordon: trombone, Lennox Brown: alto saxophone, Earl 'Chinner' Smith: lead guitar, Robert 'Robbie' Shakespeare: bass & Carlton 'Santa' Davis: drums
[5] 'Double Barrel' – Dave Barker & Ansel Collins – Wind (Jamaica)/Techniques TE 901 (UK) 7" 1970 A Number One UK hit
[6] 'The Night Doctor' – The Upsetters – Upsetter (Jamaica & UK US 307) 7" 1969
[7] 'Flat Foot Hustling': *"a flat foot hustler is a self made man… a man who can go out and make things happen"* Bunny 'Striker' Lee

on when he came from Canada with a drummer named Joe Isaacs. Everybody wanted a cut off of that... there are about one hundred different versions 'pon it! Plenty of people don't know... the original 'Shank I Sheck' is King Edwards The Giant[1] and you know Chiang Kai-shek was a Chinese general[2]? He was a great general so Edwards named the tune 'Shank I Sheck' after him. Jackie Mittoo[3] and his band came down from Canada to Jamaica and Jackie brought down this band... he had some very good musicians who used to play with Lyn Taitt... like Joe Isaacs on drums and Brian Atkinson on bass... a guy named Carl Harvey on guitar and Lord Tanamo[4] as the vocalist. So Jackie came down with a very strong band but the show didn't take off as they expected... it wasn't promoted right.

So I started carrying those guys to the studio... it was at Joe Gibbs studio... and we decided to make 'Shank I Sheck' over but the trumpeter who was supposed to come and play it... Bobby Ellis who did it for Mrs Pottinger[5]... we never got round to put in his part. Everyone liked it and jumped on it. Every singer, every deejay and every youth producer wanted a cut off of it. But through it was so popular I did just park it for a while... I give you a cut of it and you give a next man a cut of it and so it goes on... you know? Sugar Minott made a hit 'pon it and when me hear Sugar Minott 'pon it in England[6] I asked him *"Where did you get that rhythm?"* and he said *"A friend of yours... Professor[7]... gave me a cut of it"*. Tubby called it 'Flat Foot Hustling' 'cause every little man come and wanted a cut off of it. Every man would beg *"Boy, Striker you have a rhythm that me like... give me a cut of it now"*. So every man a voice a tune 'pon it but we then made them do it for themselves 'cause too many people were flat foot hustling for it.

Lloyd Charmers was like my partner... Charmers and Glen Adams. If I was going out on the road and had a session to run I'd leave either Lloyd Charmers or Glen Adams in charge... remember Charmers was a musician as well as a singer. I could leave Lloyd Charmers in charge of a session and go away...

---

[1] 'Shank I Sheck' – Baba Brooks – King Edwards (Jamaica)/Rio R 61 (UK) 7" 1965

[2] Chiang Kai-shek: President of The Republic of China (Taiwan) 1948 to 1975

[3] Jackie Mittoo: Donat Roy 'Jackie' Mittoo Born 3rd March 1948. Died 16th December 1990. Jackie's towering influence on the development of Jamaican music through his work at Studio One, where he helped to build, refine and define the sound of reggae as a musician, composer and arranger, is truly remarkable but he has remained a background figure to all but serious students of Jamaican music

[4] Lord Tanamo: Joseph Abraham 'Lord Tanamo' Gordon: singer

[5] 'Shank I Sheck' - Bobby Ellis & The Revolutionaries – High Note (Jamaica) 7" 1977

[6] 'African Girl' – Sugar Minott – Live & Love LLDIS 113 (UK) 12" 1980

[7] Professor: Winston 'Professor' Brown: recording engineer at King Tubby's studio

come back and everything was alright. You remember the original 'Penny For Your Song'[1]? It was a calypso band playing it[2]... a band from Victoria Market down at the bottom of King Street. Charmers and me were down West Indies Records and see these guys trying to make the tune and he stopped them and said *"You need a keyboard man!"* and so they asked Charmers and Charmers a play it. The next thing I know it's a very big hit! That time Scotty[3] was in the group and another guy... three of them... The Federals. They did it over several times but they never get the vibe like we did get with the calypso band. So Charmers is a singer in his own right... he used to lead The Charmers group from ska days. He was part of the Flames with Alton Ellis... yeah man. Charmers is around a long time and he's a very good producer... one of the best. He did 'Everything I Own' with Ken Boothe[4] and after he went on his own... he did a lot of things... Lloyd Charmers... he's one of the best producers from Jamaica... in any language.

There used to be a rivalry between Tommy McCook and Roland Alphonso about who was the best sax man. But when you wanted a good session you had all of them on board. You have another guy named Karl Bryan... we call him King Cannon[5]. And Lester Sterling! You had every man and every man played on the same rhythm and each man try and better the other man.

Duke Reid used to have a musician named Marquis[6]... he used to play with Burning Spear[7] in the Seventies... he had a big baritone sax. Tommy McCook and Marquis used to do the arrangements and Byron Smith was Duke Reid's engineer... another great engineer. We used to call him Smithy. He was the man who when every man said *"the tune gone!"* and Duke would fire two shots in the air and say *"Smithy, what you talking about? Play it back like this!"* and he'd stand up and everybody would listen. They used to play the tape back to the Duke and the musicians would listen out and then Marquis would jump up and say *"Yes, the boss was right. You need a seventh in there."* So I nicknamed him and called him 'Seventh'. Duke would tell the man what he wanted and

---

[1] 'Penny For Your Song' – The Federals – Scotty (Jamaica)/Island WI 3126 (UK) 7" 1968

[2] George Tucker & His Orchestra

[3] Scotty: Dave 'Scotty' Scott: Lead singer with the Federals who later enjoyed hits as deejay Scotty with Derrick Harriott and Harry 'Harry J' Johnson

[4] 'Everything I Own' – Ken Boothe – Wildflower (Jamaica)/Trojan TRO 7920 (UK) 7" 1974 A Number One UK hit

[5] King Cannon: Carl 'Cannonball'/'King Cannon' Bryan: saxophone

[6] Marquis: Herman 'Seventh' Marquis: alto saxophone, baritone saxophone and musical arranger

[7] Burning Spear: Winston 'Burning Spear' Rodney: consistently successful roots reggae singer and songwriter who broke through onto the international stage in 1975 with the epochal 'Marcus Garvey' album

then go back down to his liquor store and if they made a mistake he'd come back up. He knew what he wanted. Yeah man. That was Duke.

I was doing over a Duke Reid tune one time and the musicians couldn't get the introduction right and I said to Winston Wright... who was one of my favourite musicians... he played on 'The Liquidator'[1] but he never got the credit... *"Winston you played most of Duke's tunes... you know Duke Reid never leave out a seventh."* The musicians started to argue and say this and that and Winston was there 'pon the keyboard and he just said *"You know you're right Striker. Come gentlemen. It's a seventh it needs"* and we just cut the tune. You understand?

They've left the John Crow skank out of the history of the music too because they don't understand it. Bob Marley's tune 'Duppy Conqueror'[2] it was my set of musicians that played that too: Family Man, Carlie and Glen Adams. It had the creep organ which sounded a little more refined if you did it at Dynamics as Randy's organ[3] was a tone out and you'd hear it still in (sings) *"Scharpeeee"* like on 'Stick By Me'[4]. It's still there but it isn't dominant. Randy's studio was the best studio for the John Crow skank but people don't talk about it. 'Cool Operator'[5], 'Better Must Come', Bob Marley's 'Duppy Conqueror' and 'Who Is Mr. Brown'[6] all those tunes where you hear the creep organ are the John Crow skank... and a man would say *"Play John Crow skank!"* and it reached Dynamic too. Dynamic had a good organ[7] so all them Hopeton Lewis tunes like 'Grooving Out On Life'[8] is all shuffle and creep. Once you hit with a sound you know everybody follows... the man in a dance wanted to hear this new sound... it threw the rhythm right out of place so that's how the John Crow skank did come in. Eventually it stayed with the reggae but the creep was more refined on Byron Lee's organ. It did come like salt! You have coarse salt and fine salt. You understand?

You have a next drummer called Lloyd Adams we called Tin Leg who played on 'Better Must Come'[9] and all that.... he played on 'Cherry Oh Baby' too.

---

[1] 'Liquidator' – Harry J All Stars – Harry J (Jamaica & UK TR 675) 1969 A Number Nine UK hit
[2] 'Duppy Conqueror' – Bob Marley & The Wailers
– Upsetter (Jamaica & UK US 348 & 349) 7" 1970
[3] Randys organ: a Hammond B3
[4] 'Stick By Me' – John Holt – Jackpot (Jamaica & UK JP 772) 7" 1971
[5] 'Cool Operator' – Delroy Wilson – Jackpot (Jamaica & UK JP 769) 7" 1971
[6] 'Who Is Mr Brown'/'Mr Brown' – Bob Marley & The Wailers
- Upsetter (Jamaica & UK US 354) 7" 1970
[7] Dynamic had a good organ: a Lowrey Lincolnwood DeLuxe
[8] 'Grooving Out On Life' – Hopeton Lewis – Merritone (Jamaica)/Dragon DRA 1011 (UK) 7" 1973
[9] 'Better Must Come' – Delroy Wilson – Justice (Jamaica)/Jackpot JP 763 (UK) 7" 1971

He had a different style. Tin Leg went to Duke Reid and tried it on and Duke bust two shots and never saw him again! *"Bam! Bam! In a the drum booth!"* He said *"Mr Reid me just go a toilet. Me soon come, Sir."* And all now he don't come back! Duke Reid said *"Bunny. Where'd you get that drummer?"* He went to America. He plays with The Wailers Band when they go out and play the Bob Marley songs… they use different people. He lives in California I think… Lloyd Adams. In Duke's studio there was a little speaker box that was connected up to the liquor store and if a tune was being recorded that made everybody dance the musicians would say: *"It's gone like the wheel off a Herbie[1]"*. So when they did a tune and a man says *"It's gone like the wheel off a Herbie"* that means it's a runaway hit!

Winston Grennan was a kind of underdog drummer 'cause Hugh Malcolm was playing with Jackie Jackson for Beverley's and all that. Grennan married Val Bennett's big daughter and she have a child for him. He started this one drop thing. In those days we used to call it … excuse my language… the cow shit splash (sings) *"People get ready to do, do rock steady… splash!"* Now it's come like they call it the one drop but it's the cow shit splash… you know like when the cow dung drops? In those days the cows used to walk plenty in Jamaica… in the bush or on the road… and you'd hear the cow dung splash. Pow! The engineer used to complain and say *"Boy… this drummer's foot is too heavy and him mash up me needle…"* but we didn't discard it and let it run. I used to say *"Winston I want you to play the cow shit splash! Heh, heh, heh"* and then I'd say *"Lynford from it nah distort just take the tune same way. You understand?"* Because Lynford Anderson was a good engineer and he used to watch the needles but when Winston's drum dropped they'd go badly into the red! He was the master at that, man…

But Grennan is one of the greats… he used to work for the government at Kingston Corporation behind Tivoli Gardens and when he got time off he'd pack up his drum set in the back of his car and come and say *"Striker… I want you to run a session today. I nah go work today! I feel fit! We have to pick up Bobby Aitken and go a studio… get some studio time! I feel like playing the drums today…"* Sometimes he'd come with a whistle! He did love it man! That time I used to be in charge of the studio down at WIRL and he'd go and pick up all of the musicians and come back. We had a bass man named Vincent White… he played on 'My Conversation' and things like that. He played on a lot of hit tunes but plenty people don't talk about him. He used to be in Bobby Aitken's band… Bobby Aitken & The Carib Beats.

---

[1] Herbie: Walt Disney's 'The Love Bug', the top grossing film of 1969, starred a Volkswagen Beetle motor car named Herbie with a mind of its own that became a championship racer

I was talking about Winston Grennan. He's another man who taught Sly when Sly used to watch him... he was one of Sly's mentors. Sly used to come from school and watch Grennan play. Sly will tell you if you ask him this. Him come one time to play a session and Grennan say *"Youth! Finish your school and work. School important. So come back in the evening. Take in your school... school important."*

Santa[1] was a great drummer. He started with The Soul Syndicate[2]. He wore size fourteen shoes and that's why when he licked the drum it sound! It was a pleasure to watch him work. Sly played the drums so brilliant but he played different from Santa... Santa went on to play with Peter Touch[3]... he even got shot with Peter Touch. He lives in California now. Peter Touch used to work with me at one time as a musician... play guitar and organ and sing harmony because in those days I used to pay the artists twenty pounds a week. I was making 'nough money from sales of the records and if a man got twenty pounds a week he could pay his rent, buy his food and look after his kids. I used to see that every artist go alright! If a man had problems with his kids going to school... well... they'd soon find me! Some of them did records for me... you understand? But that's why I probably don't have any money today!

Cornell Campbell's 'The Stal A Wat'[4] was the first time I tested out Sly on drums on that session... because Cornell is a good bass man, you know, and he used to have his band in Spanish Town... I think Horace Andy was playing the guitar... three men played 'pon it. A police friend of mine came up with the idea... it's a kind of take off of 'Cherry Oh Baby' but a different sound. One Saturday I went to Channel One[5] with four people: me, Cornell Campbell, Horace Andy and somebody else I can't remember... it's the keyboard man I can't remember but a keyboard man was there with me. I said *"Sly I'd like you to play 'pon a tune for me"*. He said *"What we a go make over?"* and I said *"Let's lick over 'Cherry Oh Baby' in your stepping style"*.

---

[1] Santa: Carlton 'Santa' Davis: drums

[2] The Soul Syndicate: superb Seventies session band that included drums: Carlton 'Santa' Davis, bass: George 'Fully' Fullwood, rhythm guitar: Albert Valentine 'Tony' Chin, lead guitar: Earl 'Chinna' Smith & Albert Valentine 'Tony' Chin, keyboards: George 'Fully' Fullwood, Bernard 'Touter' Harvey & Keith Sterling and vocalists: Dennis Brown, Freddie McGregor & Earl Zero

[3] Peter Touch: Winston Hubert McIntosh, also known as Peter Tosh, one of the original Wailers. Born 19th October 1944. Shot dead in his home 11th September 1987. Wilton 'Doc' Brown and Jeff 'Free I' Dixon were also shot dead in the incident. Santa was injured.

[4] 'The Stal A Wat' – Cornell Campbell – Jackpot (Jamaica) 7" 1976

[5] Channel One Recording Studio, 29 Maxfield Avenue, Kingston 13

Cornell sang 'The Stal A Wat' 'pon it and Jah Stitch deejayed 'No Man Can't Dead With The Dread Upon Him Head'[1] 'pon that rhythm too. It was a Barry Brown tune that he'd sung. You never hear the Barry Brown one? You never hear that tune? I'm going to look for it... it's a rare tune man. So when Stitch got shot he was in the hospital and as soon as I could I take him out of the hospital and use the topic and come up with the tune. We used that title now and said *"Jah Stitch! You did get shot so come out of yourself now! No man can't dead with the dread 'pon him head"* and the rest is history. 'Cause he got shot and everybody said Jah Stitch was dead and everything so I said *"No man can't dead with the dread 'pon him head..."* but it was really Barry Brown's words that me use 'cause Barry Brown sing it... we just carried Jah Stitch 'pon the rhythm.

So Sly played the drums, Cornell played the bass... he is an ace bass man too... and Horace played the guitar. I went into the control room and said *"The drum is hard. It's the heart of this session"* and so I asked Sly if he could do one more session for me. *"But don't tell me no! I have a John Holt session tomorrow. You'll be playing with Robbie"*. The next day was Sunday. So I got up went to the studio and the musicians all came and it was first time Sly and Robbie played drum and bass together. Before that it was Sly and Ranchie[2] or Lloyd Sparks[3]. Robbie was my bass man but I said *"No matter. You can work with anybody!"*

There were no keyboards just Chinna[4] with Sly and Robbie and a guy called Bo Peep[5] who used to play with Lloyd Sparks. Pure hits came out of that session. I remember when Jo Jo[6] came into the studio and he looked 'pon the piano and the organ as he's heard an organ sound and a kind of piano sound and he can't see nobody. He said *"Where's the keyboard man then Striker?"* and I said to Jo Jo *"He's invisible!"* But it was the wah wah guitar that we dropped from Chinna. He shuffled 'pon the guitar like it's an organ... just listen to the records! John Holt sang 'I Forgot To Say I Love You'... a Chi-Lites tune [7], 'Winter World Of Love', 'In The Springtime', 'Let's Get It While It's Hot'...

---

[1] 'No Dread Can't Dead' – Jah Stitch – Third World TWS 401 (UK) LP 1976
[2] Ranchie: Bertram 'Ranchie' McLean: guitar & bass
[3] Lloyd Sparks: Lloyd 'Sparks' Parks: bass, singer, musical arranger, band leader and record producer
[4] Chinna: Earl 'Chinna' Smith: guitar, musical arranger and record producer
[5] Bo Peep: Winston 'Bo Peep' Bowen: guitar
[6] Jo Jo: Joseph 'Jo Jo' Hookim: Chinese Jamaican entrepreneur, record producer and proprietor of Channel One Recording Studio. Jo Jo's labels included Channel One, Disco Mix, Hit Bound & Well Charge
[7] 'I Forgot To Say I Love You Till I'm Gone'
– The Chi-Lites – 'The Chi-Lites' - Brunswick (USA) LP 1973

we made a whole LP that Sunday morning. It came out as '3000 Volts Of Holt'[1]. Trojan put it out... John Holt platted up his hair 'pon the sleeve!'

Then after Sunday's session I said *"Boy! You sound good Sly! Come in! I want you to work on Monday along with Robbie on bass for Johnny Clarke"*. So Sly came in again and he wrote a tune for Johnny named 'Want-e Want-e Can't Get It'[2]. Jackie Mittoo was on that rhythm too. That was one of the tunes that carried Jah Stitch to England. He called it 'Aggrovating Version'[3] and we called that like a top ranking sound now! On Sunday Sly & Robbie did the John Holt LP and on Monday they did the Johnny Clarke LP and from then on they never looked back because when those tunes came out they just ran and ran.

But The Revolutionaries didn't only work at Channel One. I used to work with them at Harry J's[4] because I used every musician! You needed to do that because of some of the songs. Sometimes I'd have a song... for instance John Jolt used to live beside me and every day I'd hear him sing this tune 'You'll Never Find'[5] so I put it on a tape and said to Sly *"I have a tune"* and so I asked Lloyd[6] *"I want you to make to make the rhythm in a g for me"* and I gave him and Sly the tape. The keyboard player was a disabled guy we called Tarzan[7]. Bad! Ansel Collins hummed the tune and they made the rhythm. And then I carried it to Harry J's to voice it. Now Lloyd Sparks is a great bass man and him have a good band now[8]. He's stayed the test of time! But we also had Robbie, Family Man and when I did over a Wailers tune that's why they were so authentic. On Johnny Clarke's 'Crazy Bald Head'[9] it's the same Family Man who played bass on Bob Marley's original version[10]. Bob couldn't stop them because it's through me why they got to know him anyway!

---

[1] '3000 Volts Of Holt' – John Holt – Trojan TRLS 143 (UK) LP 1977
[2] 'Want-e Want-e Can't Get It' – Johnny Clarke – Weed Beat (Jamaica) 7" 1975
[3] 'Aggrovating Version' – Jah Stitch – Attack (Jamaica) 7" 1975
[4] Harry J Recording Studio, 10 Roosevelt Avenue, Kingston 6
[5] 'You'll Never Find Another Love Like Mine'
– Lou Rawls – Philadelphia International (USA) 7" 1976
[6] Lloyd: Lloyd 'Sparks' Parks
[7] Tarzan: Errol 'Tarzan' Nelson: keyboards
[8] Lloyd Parks & The We The People Band
[9] 'Crazy Bald Head' – Johnny Clarke – Justice (Jamaica)/Virgin VS 159 (UK) 7" 1977
[10] 'Crazy Baldhead' – Bob Marley & The Wailers
– 'Rastaman Vibration' Tuff Gong (Jamaica)/Island ILPS 9383 (UK) LP 1976

Sly played the flying cymbals first... I said to Sly *"You played it on the Delroy Wilson tune for Channel One named 'It's A Shame'[1]"* and Sly played it before that with Skin, Flesh & Bones on 'Here I Am Baby Come And Take Me'[2], the Al Green tune, when Al Brown[3] sung it for Dickie Wong with the *"tsk, tsk, tsk"* sound on the hi-hat. I named it flyers[4] but they didn't know what flyers was! It's not the right name really. Anytime I did a session I used to get loads of Kentucky Fried Chicken for the musicians and when it came they'd say *"put up the flyers for Striker"* meaning the wings, which I loved, and they used to say *"Striker. When you a go fly?"* And everybody started to get puzzled when Johnny Clarke hit with this flyers. Yeah... I used to eat the chicken wings and I said *"Santa I want something that sound like it's come from outer space!"*

Chris Blackwell was in trouble now because he had a lot of money 'pon Bob Marley! Bob Marley's 'No Woman No Cry'[5] came out. Rita Marley's version[6] came out but they couldn't stop Johnny Clarke's version[7] selling! It was a hit all round the Caribbean. Chris had to get Carl Gayle[8] to write about *"this boring flying cymbals and this thing there"*. Yeah man... but we gave Carl Gayle some of his stories... John Holt and myself![9]

After Family Man went to play for The Wailers I took over Robbie Shakespeare as my bass man. I used him... 'Fully'[10] sometimes and Bagga[11]. Then Bob Marley did send Carlie to come 'mongst we... 'cause Carlie started out with me first... through the flyers was giving them such a hard time and no man knew

---

[1] 'It's A Shame' – Delroy Wilson – Well Charge (Jamaica) 7" 1975 *"The disco thing started to come in 1975 and there was not a lot of work for live bands so I started to concentrate more on the studio work. The first session I played for Channel One was Delroy Wilson's version to The Spinners' 'It's A Shame'. It was a big hit for Jo Jo".* Sly Dunbar

[2] 'Here I Am (Come And Take Me)' – Al Green – Hi (USA) 7" 1973

[3] 'Here I Am Baby Come And Take Me' – Al Brown & Skin, Flesh & Bones Inc – Tit For Tat (Jamaica)/Trojan TR 7935 (UK) 7" 1973

[4] flyers: style of rhythm based around the Philadelphia disco sound also termed flying cymbals (the sound of an open and closed hi-hat) and **the** sound of 1974/1975. Johnny Clarke's interpretation of Earl Zero's 'None Shall Escape The Judgement' - Justice (Jamaica)/Explosion EX 2089 (UK) 7" 1974 was one of the first, and biggest, hits in Striker's flyers style

[5] 'No Woman No Cry' (live) – Bob Marley & The Wailers - Island WIP 6244 (UK) 7" 1975 & 'No Woman No Cry' – Bob Marley & The I Threes & Wailers – Tuff Gong (Jamaica) 7" 1975

[6] 'No Woman No Cry' – I Threes – Tuff Gong (Jamaica) 7" 1975

[7] 'No Woman No Cry' – Johnny Clarke – Justice (Jamaica)/Grounation GRO 2003 (UK) 7" 1975

[8] Carl Gayle: influential, insightful staff writer for *'Black Music'* magazine. *"This flying cymbals sound that Bunny Lee, the producer, is so proud of makes this number unattractive..."* *Black Music* Volume 3 Issue 26 January 1976

[9] Carl Gayle: 'Dem Dread Out Deh' *Black Music* Vol. 2 Issue 20 July 1975
Carl Gayle: 'Oh, What A Rat Race' *Black Music* Vol. 3 Issue 31 June 1976

[10] Fully: George 'Fully' Fullwood: bass

[11] Bagga: Earl 'Bagga' Walker: bass

what the flyers was. So Carlie did come and said *"Bunny. The boss want to fire me... what is flyers?"* and I said *"Carlie. I'll tell you what flyers is and I'll make you play it too. I'm going to make you play on this tune here. Santa! Show him what flyers is... the open cymbal. You're going to play it!"*

'Gorgon' was a tune... make I tell you now... it was a tune that Derrick Morgan did... 'Conquering Ruler'[1]. I had a friend and he used to say *"Boy the man there a gorgon..."* it meant he was the champion. Derrick write the tune off of his tune and I said *"Cornell I want you to sing it"*. On 'Gorgon'[2] it's Bagga... that's Bagga Walker... him get him bass and go into it... Jah Jerry[3] and Carlie played the drums. Chinna brought the great guitarist from the Skatalites named Jah Jerry 'cause he was showing Chinna how the ska went.

This was Harry J's studio now and Jah Jerry came in and I said *"Jah Jerry... you have to play 'pon one tune now"*. He was to play the ska but he couldn't keep the timing right so I said *"Jah Jerry... hear what you're going to do now. You're going to play the lead guitar, the intro, the solo and the ending part. That good you know!"* and some of the musicians started *"Ray, ray, ray..."* and I said *"Them man paved the way for we. If it wasn't for them we wouldn't have no music. If a man like Jah Jerry's not going to play 'pon the session then we'll stop the session right here and now"*. Chinna said *"Gentlemen! You no hear what Mr Lee said? Jerry? Mr Lee say you must stay!"* and then Jerry came up with an intro and his pretty little solo and that tune is a classic all now... 'Gorgon'. You understand? Everyone laughed and said *"Bob Marley can't find the flyers! He's sent Carlie out to check"* but I said *"Me a go tell you Carlie 'cause you are my original drummer"*.

Sly had played it first but he never realised what he had and because I loved my chicken wings we just named it flyers (sings) *"tsk, tsk, tsk, tsk..."* We carried them to Tubbys to mix the tunes and passed it through the high pass filter[4] on his machine where he pushed up one of the things on his board and it thinned it out. Styled it out man! (sings) *"tsk, tsk, tsk, tsk..."* It took on!

---

[1] 'Conquering Ruler' – Derrick Morgan – Hop (Jamaica)/Island WI 3094 (UK) 7" 1968

[2] 'Gorgon'/'The Mighty Gorgon' – Cornell Campbell
– Attack (Jamaica)/Klik KL 607 (UK) 7" 1975

[3] Jah Jerry: Jerome 'Jah Jerry' Haynes aka Hines Born 5th May 1927. Died 13th August 2007. Foundation guitarist best known for his work with The Skatalites

[4] high pass filter: *"The effect has variously been described as a phase shifter and an equaliser but it is, in fact, a sophisticated high pass filter: a type of tone control designed to remove whole portions of unwanted bass frequencies from material sent through it. The control has several notches, so that you can hear the separate frequencies disappearing when the knob is being twisted, and a very steep filter slope which induces the phasing effect on the remaining material"* Chris Lane

Dave Hendley

Jo Jo Hookim at Channel One

TRAIN TO SKAVILLE

RIO

R 130 A
Wirl

ETHIOPIANS

DIRECT RECORDS LTD

TiT for TaT

TIME
4.00
Phone
42071

A D
W
PRODUC
℗ 19

HERE I AM BABY
COME AND TAKE ME
(AL GREEN)
AL BROWN
SKIN, FLESH AND BONES INC

JUSTICE

45 RPM

Produced by   Distributed by

This a the best
VERSION
The Agrovators

TROGAN'S

PRODUCED
BY
B. LEE

45 R P M

My Baby Just Care For Me
Cornell Campbell

MADE FROM MASTER RECORDINGS OF MUDIE'S RECORDS

AFRO

DISTRIBUTED BY
H. MUDIE

HM1011A

TIME 2"58

IF I DID KNOW

ROY SHIRLEY

COXSONE
RECORDS

Made In Ja.

MADE IN JAMAICA

Jamrec Mus

MY GUIDING STAR
JOE WHITE

128

Chapter 15 King Tubby's Version... The Dub Master

And we didn't reach Tubbys[1] yet...

Tubby's Sound was a little sound... a village hometown hi-fi... Tubby's Home Town Hi-Fi like Chappy's Home Town Hi Fi or Jammy's Home Town Hi Fi... and me and Tubbys really take up a friendship. The first time we voiced in Tubbys was when we were going to play a sound[2].

We started dub with King Tubbys but the man who really pushed version was U Roy[3] and Ruddys from Spanish Town... but through him don't come to town[4]

---

[1] Tubbys: Osbourne 'King Tubby' Ruddock also known as Tubbs or Tubbys. Born January 28th 1941. Died February 6th 1989. The importance of King Tubby's Home Town Hi Fi and King Tubby's studio to the development of Jamaican music can never be overstated: the music emanating from his Waterhouse studio became a world wide phenomenon. King Tubby 'The Dub Master' transformed not only the music making process but also the way that music was listened to and understood in the latter half of the twentieth century

[2] *"Striker was the man who come and saw Tubbs with his little mixing board and said 'Let's start a studio'. They didn't even have no proper voicing facilities but Striker say 'Yes. We can do it here' so they hook up a microphone and just work like that."* King Jammy

[3] U Roy: Ewart 'U Roy' Beckford: deejay

[4] come to town: come to Kingston

plenty of people don't know of him. Taking the voice from the rhythm... Tubbys now and Ruddys... we're talking one argument. But Tubbys and me had really met upstairs at Duke Reid's one day when the version thing came in... it was a mistake made up at Duke Reid's studio. One day we were at Duke's studio and Tubby came up to cut some dub[1] with Ruddy. Now Ruddys was really the man that started playing version... we called it version not drum and bass. Ruddys was a big businessman and he had a big club in Spanish Town named Big Daddy... he had a club by the seaside too across the water in Port Henderson. He was a wealthy man... he had racehorses and a record shop. When Ruddys from Spanish Town came to Coxsone's or Duke Reid's studio they gave him the keys to the city and allowed him to use **any** tape because his sound was like a big radio station in Spanish Town... anything that Ruddys played the other sound men wanted it and then the record buying people too.

Tubbys and myself was there talking and Ruddys was cutting a dub and Smithy[2] forgot to put in the voice through we were talking and he was going to stop it. Ruddys said *"No! Make it run. Let it stay..."* and so they cut the pure rhythm. When it finished they cut it back on the other side and when they were done they cut the one with the voice... started it over again with the singing right through. It was two track recording in those days. I never took any notice of it. Me and Tubbys were just sitting there. Now Tubbys wanted some rhythms to play on his sound of 'Ain't Too Proud To Beg'[3] and we drove over to Greenwich Farm to pick up the tapes.

I used to go over and listen to Ruddys sound and Stereo's sound in Spanish Town... in those days Spanish Town was nicer than it is now. That Saturday night a dance was in progress and when they played the vocal to the tune... I don't remember whose tune it was but it was Alton Ellis or John Holt they were playing... then Wasp the deejay said *"me a go play part two"*. They never called it version and then he played the rhythm track. The song was a catchy song and everybody started to sing. The people just caught the song and sang it over the rhythm. They must have played it about five or ten times and it brought down the house or... as we say in Jamaica... it mashed up the place!

On the Monday I met Tubbys at Duke Reid's... Duke would let Tubbys take anything he wanted to cut... and I said *"Tubbys... you know the mistake we made upstairs at Duke's studio? It's a serious joke, you know, because the people them love it".* So I said to Tubbs *"It's a serious thing. It mash up*

---

[1] cut some dub: make an acetate/reference disc
[2] Smithy: Byron 'Smithy'/'Baron' Smith: recording engineer at Treasure Isle Recording Studio
[3] 'Ain't Too Proud To Beg' – Slim Smith – Unity (Jamaica & UK UN 515) 7" 1969 also 'Too Proud To Beg' – The Uniques – Gas GAS 117 (UK) 7" 1969

Spanish Town. The people went wild. So we'll have to start to do some of that. You have to start to do that now". 'Cause when the man put on the part two everyone start singing this song… it played about twenty times so I said *"you try Tubbs!"*

So Tubbs cut several versions of the Slim Smith 'Ain't Too Proud To Beg'… Lester Sterling, U Roy and Roland Alphonso. Slim Smith sing a next tune 'pon it 'Keep That Light'[1]. Well the next Saturday night now when Tubbys strung up down Greenwich Farm[2] U Roy said he's going to play part two but Tubbys did it different now. Tubbs was a man who improvised. He started with the voice then dropped it out and let the rhythm run and then he brought in the voice in the middle. On Slim Smith's tune you'd hear Slim Smith start to sing and then he'd just take out Slim Smith's voice and bring in the (sings) *"boom booda boom, boom boom boom"* and we had about five or six different cuts of that tune.

When Tubbys started doing it he left a little bit of the voice in and then he dropped it out and it take on so we started! The people started going round saying *"Boy! Tubbys have an amplifier that is the greatest. It takes out the voice and leaves the pure rhythm"*. Then the word started to get out saying Tubbys had an amplifier that can take out the voice and everybody started looking. But they didn't know that the trick was to start with the voice and then take out the voice and bring in the rhythm and then later on he'd bring in a little of the voice. People started asking about it. Even Vincent Chin from Randy's came after him… *"Boy. What kind a thing is this? I hear Tubby have an amp that can drop the voice out of the record"*. So I said *"Vincent. It's a gyow[3] but I don't know how you got to hear about it. You just start off with the voice and bring in the rhythm and then bring back the voice… sometimes you bring in the voice with no rhythm and you just hear the singer on the soft wax[4]"*. But the people believed it was the amplifier that did it!

And from there Tubbys started to get really popular. We couldn't afford for every song to get a different set of musicians so we started using the same rhythm over again. We did a next tune and Niney carried it to U Roy and he said *"Awoah! Another version of the tune!"* As I told you Niney is a quick man and he told me *"Striker! The new name now is version… U Roy just told me about it!"* That's how the name version a come in. You understand? Niney told me as he was the man who came and said U Roy said *"Another version of the tune!"*

---

[1] 'Keep That Light' – Slim Smith – Jackpot (Jamaica)/Unity UN 537 (UK) 7" 1969
[2] Greenwich Farm: Kingston 13
[3] gyow: false/untrue
[4] soft wax: reference disc/acetate/dub

Before that they used to play part one, part two, part three and go right up. I said *"Boy it sound good"* and from that everybody said *"we play version"* until U Roy come and start saying 'Version Galore'[1] with Duke Reid.

When Tubbys started with his amplifier thing I had the Bunny Lee Radio Show... Bunny Lee and Randy's A Go Go... and I used to advertise Tubbys on it: *"If you want your dub and all the latest discs and thing check King Tubbys".* In those days I never used to put the version on the record so you'd have to go to Tubbys sound to hear the dub play... it took off and then the people started wanting it on their records. Tubbys was the place now and I used to keep all of my tapes up there and all the guys used to come to Tubbys. Everybody started coming to Tubby's studio... it was a little room and a bathroom set up. We started to voice tunes at Tubbys... do the rhythm at Dynamics then we voice it at Tubbys. He started to get popular and I started to get Tubbys to mix and use him as an engineer.

We started to put out tunes with a version on... people used to want to hear the version... but Tubbs used to say make them come to him for the version! Because the first time I stood up in Randys and a man played 'Queen Of The Minstrel'[2] with Cornell and turned it over... no version! I always gave the people value for money... two big sides... but it never go like that now. Them no want that. The man them wanted the version 'cause when they no hear the version they'd walk and leave it. So from that we just started to deal with the version and put it behind the record.

So the sound men started flocking to Tubbys for a different cut... their style... every man! Now you can get the same thing through the computer ... you log it in to the computer and all you have to do is press a button and you get the same thing you did get thirty... forty years ago but them days you'd have to mix it. Every cut is a different cut you know... it's a different feel. Even if you have two dubs it can't sound the same way... it might be a similar rhythm but a different vibes... 'cause it was a man doing it in those days. Either he'd put more echo or more of the squawking effect *"swwwt, swwwt, swwwt..."* the high pass filter you know. First time we do that Tubbys said *"It's madness!"* and then they listened it back and he couldn't believe it when they tried it on the sound system crowd! So they started using it... the high pass filter... and Tubbys studio became so in demand that not even me could get studio time now! I'd have to wait until late at night because everybody was coming and

---

[1] 'Version Galore' – U Roy – Treasure Isle (Jamaica)/Duke Reid DR 2515 (UK) 7" 1970
[2] 'Queen Of The Minstrel' – Cornell Campbell – Jackpot (Jamaica) 7" 1972

wanted Tubbys to mix their tunes until Pablo[1] bring Phillip Smart[2] down there and Phillip Smart started work... then Jammys then Scientist[3] and then Professor[4].

You'd hear plenty of tunes that drop out ... you'd hear a man sing and you just dropped out the rhythm and *"chinnng!"* and style it up. I used to do that when you had a guy who sang off key! He'd start on key but when he reached a corner he'd sing it straight as the rhythm changed. Tubbys would say *"It can't work man!"* but I said *"Yeah Tubbs! When we reach that bridge we'll cross it!"* So Tubbs set it up and I'd say *"You go on and control the bass part and the thing with the guitar but when you reach there so just drop out the guitar and bring in the drum and pure noise and then drop out the bass and chiiinnnggg!"* When you listened back to it... it's a sound... and it became a hit! So everybody started doing it now but they didn't know it was through the singer was off key. They thought it was a style and everybody followed we and started the drop outs! You understand? We started with all the things and you'd hear the bass come in but it's through the singer came in out of time or off key but with the pure drum track alone it nah really go off key! *"Boof, boof, boof"* and you bring in *"Chiinngggg, chiiinnggg"* and make the rhythm run! It worked!

It's like when I did 'Bongo Natty'[5] with Owen Gray. There was a change in it... a swinging bridge we used to call it... but Owen Gray sang it straight and Tubbys was going to stop it. I said *"No Tubbs make it go on..."* and Tubbs said *"But that can't go out so Striker!"* and I said *"Yeah man!"* so he said *"Alright... don't bother stop it man"*. And when the time came to mix it and we reached to the swinging bridge I said *"Tubbs... put the drum in delay. Drop out all the other instruments and just bring in the guitar. Ching, ing, ing...!"* Just pure madness! And he mixed it right back so when he started to sing we just brought back the full rhythm. So when Tubby listened back to it he said *"I can't believe that!"* I said *"Yes Tubbs!"* So it goes!

And everybody started to follow us and drop out the rhythm but they didn't know that when certain people come in and sing off key we'd have to drop them out because they'd gone flat... but when the drums had gone in delay it didn't show! Singing on pure drum and bass and if it ran too long you'd bring in the echo. Come back and do a whole heap of madness and plenty people started to

---

[1] Pablo: Horace 'Augustus Pablo' Swaby: Born 21st June 1953. Died 18th May 1999. Legendary, influential musician and record producer who popularised the use of the melodica in Jamaican music
[2] Phillip Smart: Phillip 'Prince Phillip' Smart: recording engineer
[3] Scientist: Overton 'Scientist' Browne: recording engineer
[4] Professor: Winston 'Professor' Brown: recording engineer
[5] 'Bongo Natty' – Owen Gray – Attack (Jamaica)/Horse HOSS 64 (UK) 7" 1975

follow we and drop out drum and bass. Drum and bass first and vocals in between… people followed that too.

So after that Tubbs started to come like an artist and we made two dub LPs with him: 'Dub From The Roots'[1] and 'The Roots Of Dub'[2] and then another LP named 'Brass Rockers'[3] with Tommy McCook playing over some of Johnny Clarke's flying cymbal rhythms. But all of those Tubbys albums that you see out on the street… most of them are frauds as it was only three albums that Tubby did… 'Dub From The Roots', 'The Roots Of Dub'… and perhaps one named 'Shalom Dub'[4]. You could call that Tubbys too because he mixed the versions but they were versions off of forty fives. Klik took it and put it out but the third is 'Brass Rockers' with Tommy McCook 'pon the flying cymbals where he mixed it with the horn going in and out in a kind of dub way but all the others a man just get something and say it's King Tubbys. Me and Tubbys used to do a whole heap of different forty fives too. They can get put together and we can call it 'Unreleased Tubbys'!

---

[1] 'Presents Dub From The Roots' – King Tubby The Dub Master - Total Sounds (Jamaica)/Live & Love TSL 106 (UK) LP 1974 & Jamaican Recordings JRCD/LP 036 2010
[2] 'Presents The Roots Of Dub' – King Tubby - Total Sounds (Jamaica)/Grounation GROL 502 (UK) LP 1975 & Jamaican Recordings JRCD/LP 035 2010
[3] 'Brass Rockers' - Bunny Lee And King Tubby Present Tommy McCook And The Aggravators - Total Sounds (Jamaica) LP 1975 & Jamaican Recordings JRCD/LP 037 2010
[4] 'Shalom Dub' – King Tubby – Klik KLP 9002 (UK) LP 1975 & Jamaican Recordings JRCD/LP 038 2010

Osbourne 'King Tubby' Ruddock

The Roots Of Dub...

Beverley's RECORDS

135ª ORANGE STREET
KINGSTON, JAMAICA. W. I.

S.R. 038

"54-46 THAT'S MY NUMBER"
(F. HIBBERT)
THE MAYTALS

MADE FROM MASTER RECORDINGS OF MUDIE'S RECORDS

AFRO

DISTRIBUTED BY
H. MUDIE

GIVE ME SOME MORE LOVING
(HARRY A. MUDIE)
SLIM SMITH & UNIQUES

JACKPOT RECORDS

B&C Music
℗ 1970

JP-733 A

D. J. CHOICE
(B. Lee)
WINSTON WILLIAMS
Produced by: Bunnie Lee

PROPHECY

Dont cut off you Dred locks
Dirval Thompson

RETIREMENT RD. KGN. 5.

BIG SHOT

PRODUCED
BY
B. Lee

45

Never Gonna Give Up
DERRICK MORGAN

ATTACK

MAGNUM FORCE
VIN GORDON AND
THE AGROVATORS

Chapter 16 Talking Version... The Deejays

I used to bring up the artists to tour in the UK because it took the pressure off of me when they earned more money on the stage shows and they'd also get some knowledge of the outside world. I brought a lot of artists up here: Leroy Smart, Johnny Clarke, Cornell Campbell, Derrick Morgan... all of those people it's me did bring them come.

I carried U Roy up to England for Mrs King... I talked about her already. She was the first person to bring U Roy to England[1] when I brought U Roy, Maxie Romeo and Roy Shirley in 1972. I did arrange the whole tour... at the same time I gave her the Slim Smith record on pre 'The Time Has Come'[2] and Slim died shortly after but she had it for a good while before that. I co-ordinated the tour and brought them all up for her. U Roy and Maxie Romeo came back home but Roy Shirley stayed until he got his residency and he never came back. It would probably have been better for him if he did visit Jamaica 'cause any time the artists stay up here they lose their roots. Even when Dennis Brown was up here for a long time I said *"D Brown... you have to go back to Jamaica. Make some tunes and when they come up here on pre you can do some shows and then go back."*

I recorded U Roy before Duke Reid, you know, with a song named 'King Of The Road'[3]. ET[4] recorded 'King Of The Road' (sings) *"Here comes the man*

---

[1] U Roy, Max Romeo and Roy Shirley toured the UK in 1972. It was U Roy's first international tour
[2] 'The Time Has Come' – Slim Smith – High Note (Jamaica)/Pama PM850 (UK) 7" 1972
[3] 'King Of The Road' – U Roy & Lennox Brown – Jackpot Blank (Jamaica)/Camel CA 038 (UK) 7" 1969 *"Now to get you in the swing of things here comes the man Lennox Brown with the big horn. He'll do for you 'The King Of The Road'"*
[4] ET: Errol 'ET'/'Errol T' Thompson

Lennox Brown with the big horn... The King Of The Road". He was a great engineer. I think he was the best engineer. He learnt his trade up at Coxsone's with Sylvan Morris[1]. And a song named 'Orgarang'[2] where I just made U Roy introduce 'Bangarang' with Lennox Brown and then another tune with Lester Sterling 'Reggae In The Wind'[3]. When he did it U Roy started in the middle and I got Jeff Barnes from the radio station... he was on both RJR and JBC... to come down and talk: *"The heights by great men reached and kept were not attained by sudden flight[4]... this brother's been in the musical fight"* till U Roy came in and then you hear the brother with *"let love shine bright along the way..."* [5] Jeff Barnes made a lot of records too but those were U Roy's first set of tunes.

Tubbys was going to play a contest one evening against Tippertone... Tubbys a fret now because Big Youth[6] and Jah Wise[7] have Tippertone Sound and they challenged him. U Roy was up in England on tour! They were supposed to have a contest over a dancehall across the water at Port Henderson a little distance out of town. So I said *"Well Tubbs no bother fret. Me have a deejay called I Roy[8]... him sound the same like U Roy. Me a go bring him in. Him up a Spanish Town. Sometimes he play a sound called Wasp, Ruddy's or Stereo"*. I Roy was also a deejay for Son's Junior from Spanish Town... I brought him in now and it was an honour for him to come and play Tubbys sound. Everybody a back Tippertone now and so I carried Roy Shirley and said *"Make we do some specials like 'the girl call me Joe Razor'* [9] *and all those kind of tunes"* and Scratch came and did one that said *"So you are the little boy that come to challenge the king"*. We closed the iron gate and Tubbs dubbed in this sound like you hear when a big cellar's locked. So I did leave and came back to England. I heard Tubbys beat Tippertone and I Roy beat Big Youth. I wasn't there but I Roy on Tubbys sound just get popular now. They never looked back...

---

[1] Sylvan Morris: renowned recording engineer
[2] 'Orgarang' – U Roy – Jackpot Blank (Jamaica) 7" 1969
[3] 'Reggae In The Wind' – Lester Sterling – Jackpot Blank (Jamaica)/Gas GAS 103 (UK) 7" 1969
[4] *"The heights by great men reached and kept were not attained by sudden flight..."*
Henry Wadsworth Longfellow
[5] 'Wake The Nation' - Jeff Barnes & U Roy with the Agro Band
– Jackpot(Jamaica)/Smash SMA 2313 (UK) 7" 1970
[6] Big Youth: Manley Augustus 'Big Youth' Buchanan: deejay
[7] Jah Wise: owner of Tippertone Sound
[8] I Roy: Roy 'I Roy' Reid: deejay Born 28th June 1944. Died 27th November 1999
[9] 'Joe Razor' – Roy Shirley – Soul Sound (Jamaica) 7" 1972

One time I Roy was selling more records than U Roy. I Roy took away U Roy's name and they didn't get on so well in real life. U Roy was really called I Roy[1] if you listen to 'Coming On Strong'[2] *"As the man I Roy would say..."* I Roy did take away the name and U Roy did stick with U Roy because U Roy was not dread[3] when he first started. He used to be on a sound named Dickies Dynamic before Tubbys. Dickie Wong[4] came to the UK once with Al Brown when he hit with 'Here I Am Baby'[5]. I started to do a lot of recording with I Roy too and I Roy became like one of the most famous deejays. They used to say him is the most intelligent deejay. The man used to have some great lyrics! In real life though him and U Roy never really get on. That in itself is another story. It can't be a book although it's a long story. Yeah man... U Roy and I Roy.

The man U Roy brought in the name version when he played Tubbys sound and he said to Niney *"Another version?"* Niney came to me and said *"Striker. The new thing is version!"* I hear some people have copyrighted the name version now! So you have to pay them every time you put version on your record... every time you put version on a record they get the publishing. So everything you name version they own it!

I Roy was at Tubbys studio one evening and he left and went away and Prince Jazzbo came in from round the corner with a friend of mine from Canada called George[6]. He used to come and cut specials so the artists got some money too and I used to give him the rhythms. So Jazzbo came and he couldn't do the tune and I Roy came back and said *"Jazzbo man if you was a jukebox I wouldn't put a dime into your slot'"* [7] and I said *"Tubbs take this!"* So I Roy said he was ready to voice the tune now and I said *"Oh no, no, no! It's voiced already*

---

[1] U Roy is credited as I Roy on the cover of the original Jamaican release of the 'Version Galore' album on Treasure Isle. His version to The Paragons' 'Equality & Justice' entitled 'Sound Of The Wise' is also credited to I Roy & The Paragons on Lloyd Daley's Matador label

[2] 'Coming On Strong': 'Orgarang' – U Roy – Jackpot Blank (Jamaica) 7" 1969

[3] *"U Roy is a quiet looking guy of the Rastafarian faith, a subject which he says he 'don't joke about.'"* Version Galore - Treasure Isle (Jamaica)/Trojan TBL 161 (UK) LP 1971

[4] Dickie Wong: owner of Dickies Dynamic sound system, the Tit For Tat record label and the Tit For Tat Club. *"Skin, Flesh & Bones... were the resident band at Dickie Wong's Tit For Tat Club on Red Hills Road"* Lowell 'Sly' Dunbar

[5] 'Here I Am Baby Come And Take Me' – Al Brown & Skin, Flesh & Bones Inc – Tit For Tat (Jamaica)/Trojan TR 7935 (UK) 7" 1973

[6] *"It all started when George came from Canada... he ran one of the biggest record shops in Canada* (Monica's Records, 1553 Eglington Ave. W, Toronto, Ontario) *and he wanted some singles. One from me and one from Jazzbo".* I Roy

[7] *"I had gone to King Tubby's studio. When I arrived I saw I Roy with Bunny Lee and Tapper Zukie. Tubby was preparing to voice I Roy and as he set up and balanced I Roy he pressed the record button. It started as a run down and I Roy began insulting me on the microphone. Everyone in the room laughed except me! Bunny Lee said he was going to release the tape and he did! That was the origin of the tracks"* Prince Jazzbo

Knits". We used to call I Roy Knits through him wear the knits ganzie[1] so I put out the tune[2] and Jazzbo said *"Boy. Mr Lee? What kind of joke is that?"* but I said the only thing you can do now is make back a song.

U Roy and U Brown[3] were together on Tubbys sound at that time and Jazzbo and U Brown came to me and said they wanted a rhythm so I gave him a John Holt rhythm 'A Love I Can Feel'[4] through Johnny Clarke had sung 'Do You Love Me'[5] in the flyers style for I Roy's record. So Jazzbo talked and did a tune *"I Roy you a boy. You imitate the great U Roy"* [6] and when U Roy hear the tune him laugh till him drop... so it caused a big conflict just like the Derrick Morgan and Prince Buster thing. I Roy did make back one where he said *"Jazzbo... if I did ugly like you I would take off my head and stone it."* [7]And Jazzbo came back with *"I Roy you act like girl and all them things"*. [8] I Roy came back with *"Thank you Dirty Harry! We a go a studio right now and make a tune off of it that go clap to their face... Bunny Lee and his brother in law Derrick Morgan"* where I Roy said *"he who laughs last laughs the best"*. [9] After Jazzbo came back I Roy said he was looking for *"Prince... Princess Jazzbo!"* [10] It generated some life in a the music business[11]! ... all of those things happened up at Tubbys... [12]

---

[1] knits ganzie: Italian knitwear
[2] 'Straight To Jazzbo's Head' – I Roy – Barbell & Micron (Jamaica) 7" 1975
[3] U Brown: Huford 'U Brown' Brown: deejay
[4] 'A Love I Can Feel' – John Holt – Studio One versioned over by Bunny in the flyers style as 'A Love I Can Feel' – Johnny Clarke – Barbell (Jamaica) 7" 1975
[5] 'Do You Love Me' – John Holt – Studio One versioned over by Bunny in the flyers style as 'Do You Love Me' – Johnny Clarke – Bar Bell (Jamaica) 7" 1975
[6] 'Straight To I Roy's Head' – Prince Jazzbo – Black Art (Jamaica) 7" 1975
[7] 'Jazzbo Have Fe Run' – I Roy
– Micron & Black Art (Jamaica)/Student STU 1001 (UK) 7" 1975
[8] 'Gal Boy I Roy' – Prince Jazzbo – Justice (Jamaica) 7" 1975
[9] 'Straight To Derrick Morgan's Head' – I Roy – Total Sounds (Jamaica) 7" 1975
[10] 'Padlock' – I Roy – Steady & Well Charge (Jamaica)/Dip DL 5107 (UK) 7" 1975
[11] *The whole thing was instigated by Bunny Lee... I'll show you how big this joke is. Two boxers box against I Roy now: Derrick Morgan and Jazzbo and still them couldn't win. He dealt with ignorance and I dealt with intelligence."* I Roy
[12] The entire war of words between I Roy, Prince Jazzbo and Derrick Morgan, with instrumental and vocal versions, is available on 'Once Upon A Time At King Tubbys' - Pressure Sounds PS 62 (UK) CD 2009

Tapper Zukie was my protégé and one man I see who made use of himself was Tapper Zukie[1]. Him and his brother Blackbeard started out with me and Glen Adams. Tapper joined us in the Seventies and he started by doing his own thing on the 'Guiding Star' rhythm[2]. Some guy was trying to record it... but he couldn't get it... so Tapper just went in and do it. One cut. One cut!

And Dennis AlCapone[3] is a great person. After U Roy hit Dennis AlCapone hit. Then you had another deejay named Lizzy who got big with 'Wear You From The Ball'[4]. U Roy's first tune was a tune named 'King Of The Road' with Lennox Brown. When U Roy hit with 'Wear You To the Ball'[5] Joe Gibbs got Lizzy...who was Prince Jammy's deejay... to make 'Wear You From The Ball'. Dennis was on a sound named El Paso and him come with (sings) *"A wah so? El Paso. A wah so? El Paso*[6]*..."* and people started to take on to Dennis. Me and Dennis were good friends so we started to do a lot of recording but the record that set up Dennis AlCapone was the version to 'Cherry Oh Baby'... 'Ripe Cherry'[7]... and Tyrone Downie[8] was playing that little organ thing in it. When the first 'Ripe Cherry' was released it was just the organ and Dennis AlCapone's voice... but it still sell! Every time you pass a basement you'd hear AlCapone... *"Yeah, yeah, yeah!"*... and then he did a thing named 'Buggy And Horse'[9] on 'Mule Train'[10].

---

[1] Tapper Zukie: David 'Tapper Zukie' Sinclair: highly respected deejay, record producer, record shop proprietor and entrepreneur. His debut long player 'Man Ah Warrior' – Count Shelly CSLP04/05 (UK) 1973, produced by Clem Bushay in London, is rightly regarded as a classic deejay album. He scored huge hits in England and Jamaica, as deejay and producer, with 'She Want A Phensic' – Tapper Zukie – Stars (Jamaica)/Virgin Front Line FLS 109 (UK) 7" and 'Oh Lord' – Tapper Zukie – Stars (Jamaica)/Virgin Front Line FLS 115 (UK) 7" in 1978. Tapper also produced some of the deepest roots records of the era for his Stars label with Prince Allah, Knowledge, and Junior Ross & The Spear. The classic 'Natty Dread A Weh She Want' – Horace Andy & Tapper Zukie – Stars (Jamaica) 1979/Star PTP 1020 (UK) 1980 12" was *"voted best reggae record of the year on Capital Radio and in Black Echoes"*
[2] 'Jah Is I Guiding Star' – Tapper Zukie - Dread Locks In Jamaica – Various – Live & Love LALP 05 (UK) LP 1976. A version to Striker's cut to 'Guiding Star' by Horace Andy originally 'How Can I Leave' – The Heptones – Coxsone (Jamaica) 7" 1969
[3] Dennis AlCapone: Dennis 'Dennis AlCapone' Smith: deejay
[4] 'Wear You From The Ball' – Lizzy – Jogib (Jamaica) released in the UK as 'Ten Feet Tall' – Joe Gibbs All Stars - Pressure Beat PB 5508 (UK) 7" 1970
[5] 'Wear You To The Ball' - U Roy & John Holt
– Treasure Isle (Jamaica)/Duke Reid DR 2513 (UK) 7" 1970
[6] 'Mosquito One' – El Passo (Dennis Alcapone) – Baron's (Jamaica)/Big Shot BI 572 (UK) 7" & 'El Paso' – Dennis AlCapone – Supreme (Jamaica) 7" a Studio One variation on the theme
[7] 'Ripe Cherry' – Dennis AlCapone – Jaguar J 14 (Jamaica)/Dynamic DYN 422 (UK) 7" 1971
[8] Tyrone Downie: Tyrone 'Organ D' Downie: keyboards
[9] 'Horse And Buggy' Dennis AlCapone – Jaguar (Jamaica)/Dynamic DYN 421 (UK) 7" 1971
[10] 'Mule Train' – Count Prince Miller – Jaguar (Jamaica)/Trojan TR 7824 (UK) 7" 1971

He did a lot of things and we did an album 'Al Capone's Guns Don't Argue'[1]. Byron Lee put out that album and the rest is history... but the tune that really bring him up here in England was 'Cassius Clay'[2] (sings) *"Wah wah gee wah wah..."*

[1] 'Guns Don't Argue' - Dennis AlCapone – Jaguar (Jamaica)/ Trojan TBL 187 (UK) LP 1972
[2] 'Cassius Clay' – Dennis AlCapone – Channel One (Jamaica)/Jackpot JP 808 (UK) 7" 1973

U Roy UK Tour 1972

LEE'S
45 RPM
Produced by   Distributed by
Here comes the Heart Aches
DELROY WILSON

BUNNY LEE'S
45 RPM
Produced by   Distribute
Caught You Red Handed
DELROY WILSON

STARS
Produced by
tappa zukie
dist. by
Natty Dread A Weh She
Want
HORACE ANDY
TAPPA ZUKIE
UNAUTHORISED COPYING OF THIS RECORDING IS STRICTLY PROHIBITED

SOUL SOUND
PRODUCED BY
BUNNY LEE
WHO CARES
Delroy Wilson
UNAUTHORISED COPYING PROHIBITED

SOUL SOUND
45 RPM
Produced by   istributed by
JOE RAZOR
Roy Shirley

Carib-Dis-Co
RECORD
TEL.
23725
45
R.P.M
CARIBBEAN DISTRIBUTING CO. LTD., 118 ORANGE ST., KGN., JA., W.I.

144

Chapter 17 Orange Street... Bunny Lee's Agro Record Shop

The shop in Orange Street came after Mr Rae from West Indies Records Limited gave it to me when WIRL were pulling out of the business...

The Ethiopians[1] were the first to hit the charts up here with 'Train To Skaville'[2]... Toots' biggest hit was '54-46'[3] but did you know '54-46' and 'Train To Skaville' are the same rhythm? It's just a different horn phrase. Tony Cousins and Bruce White used to run an agency to book artists[4]... they later became Desmond Dekker's managers... and The Ethiopians were the first set of guys they brought to the UK from Jamaica. The Ethiopians did that 'Train To Skaville' tune for a man named Mr Ross. He did quite a lot of recording in Jamaica with Joe White and other artists but he's dead now. You remember Joe White had a tune named 'My Guiding Star'?[5] (sings) *"I know that you're the one..."* It was on Coxsone's label but it's Mr Ross' tune. Charles Ross... yeah man... he came to Jamaica after he and his wife were just divorced... a very nice man and he made some great tunes... some big hits. 101 Orange Street was Charlie Ross' shop then he sold out and I think he did come back to England. It became Disco Land afterwards... Disco Land did buy it out... WIRL had about ten different shops all over Jamaica named Disco Land.

---

[1] The Ethiopians: hit making vocal trio featuring Leonard 'Sparrow' Dillon, Stephen Taylor & Aston Morris

[2] 'Train To Skaville' - The Ethiopians
- WIRL (Jamaica)/Rio R 130 (UK) 7" 1967 A Number Forty UK hit

[3] '54-46 That's My Number' – The Maytals
- Beverley's (Jamaica)/Pyramid PYR 6030 (UK) 7" 1968

[4] Commercial Entertainments, 4 Denmark Street (Tin Pan Alley), London WC2

[5] 'My Guiding Star' – Joe White – Coxsone (Jamaica)/Sugar ESS 102 (UK) 7" 1969

Mr Rae gave all of us a lot of chances and I get the shop when Mr Rae gave it to me... fully stocked! Mr Rae wanted to give me the presses as well but I couldn't manage pressing plants and them things... I couldn't do two things at the same time. When WIRL burned down[1] Mr Rae and a guy named Bob Gray... two army guys... kept two of the presses and set up in downtown Kingston on Chancery Lane by the side of Randy's. I couldn't manage the pressing plant because I could barely pay rent for this shop when I took it over even though Mr Rae gave it to me well stocked. So I stayed there and made myself a man out of the shop.

I had a lot of labels. Lee was my first label... just a plain little white label and then I came out with Lee's with an apostrophe s on it. I still have labels sometimes that I don't remember until I see it! Sometimes you'd just make up a label on the spur of the moment. You understand? Those days it was mainly blank labels too... did you know that you can find what the blank label records are from the matrix number? They have this book from America[2]... but sometimes even they are wrong. The blank records were alright but then the people wanted to know the name of the artists so we had the backgrounds ready and we just printed out the name. It was easier. You could just put in Jackpot or Aggrovators because in those days you used to have to do it quick!

The printer started to make them and everybody's label looked the same way but with a different name. It meant every man could do his own thing but you got out the record quicker...

Yeah man... I had Jackpot, Justice, Agro, Gas... Unity was the one that I started with Pama... then Pama Supreme... I had a lot. Attack and Jackpot over Trojan side... the Jackpot label Lee Gopthal and myself did start that, also the Big Shot label to put out my product in the UK. Trojan used Upsetter to release Lee Perry's material... Lee Gopthal gave Lee Perry the Upsetter label for his product. Roland Alphonso had Upsetter first but he wasn't putting out records so Lee Perry used it. Lee Perry did have a thing named Justice League[3] after the comics. I had one with Dynamics... they still use it now... named Jaguar.

---

[1] WIRL (West Indies Records Limited) burned down in 1969: *the factory burned which was a pressing plant... but not the offices... and not the studio because that was a separate building... separate and remote."* Graeme Goodall

[2] Michael Turner & Robert Schoenfeld: Roots Knotty Roots Nighthawk Records (USA) 2001

[3] Justice League: Justice League Of America: DC comics publication featuring, amongst others, Superman, Batman and Wonder Woman

Anything on Jaguar you know it's me who made it[1]. One named Lion through Dynamics... Dynamic had the animal labels! In the Seventies most things used to come on Jackpot... you know it was designed in Jamaica... one called Hot Stuff... Hot Shot. The first Channel One label was mine! I was the first to use it but it was a favour to Jo Jo... I used it for Delroy Wilson on 'Can I Change My Mind'[2] and 'Cassius Clay' with Dennis AlCapone The rhythm was done at Harry J's but the voicing was done at Channel One. That tune was the first recorded at Channel One... the same day we did 'Cassius Clay' with Dennis AlCapone. Dennis will tell you that.

I used to give plenty of producers tunes to put out. Those times when I first started putting out my tunes sometimes I couldn't afford to press so Prince Buster would take it over and press it. Mrs Pottinger put out some big hit tunes for me too... 'Everybody Needs Love'[3] with Slim Smith and a little after that 'The Time Has Come'[4] which was the second to last tune that Slim Smith sung. Yeah man. Mrs. Pottinger put that out. Jackie Edwards (sings) *"They took us away from Africa with the intention to steal our culture..."* [5] and 'Get Up'[6]. They were my tunes but Mrs Pottinger could get radio play so when you wanted to break an artist you gave Mrs Pottinger the tune. It wasn't about money but getting the artist to break because once they had the hit they get a name and the stage shows are going to come.

I had tunes come out on Carib-Dis-Co with Mr Robinson[7]... a Slim Smith that came out on a Mudie's label[8] and some Roy Shirley[9]. Mudies put out a John Holt LP 'Time Is the Master'[10] and five of the tracks on it are mine... 'Stick By Me', 'Looking Back', 'Riding For A Fall', 'Lost Love' and 'Oh Girl'. He got them because he and John Holt had a problem. He'd bought John Holt a car but John Holt wouldn't voice the tunes for him so I gave him some tunes to use. I gave him the two track tape and he put on strings and all that... so you'd think

---

[1] A number of Dynamic 7" labels state Produced by B. Lee. This has subsequently led to confusion as to whether the producer was Byron Lee or Bunny Lee
[2] 'Can I Change My Mind' – Delroy Wilson
– Channel One (Jamaica)/Grape GR 3038 (UK) 7" 1973
[3] 'Everybody Needs Love' – Slim Smith – High Note (Jamaica)/Unity UN 504 (UK) 7" 1969
[4] 'The Time Has Come' – Slim Smith – High Note (Jamaica)/Pama PM 850 (UK) 7" 1972
[5] 'Invasion' – Jackie Edwards – High Note (Jamaica)/Grounation GRO 2056 (UK) 7" 1975
[6] 'Get Up' – Jackie Edwards – High Note (Jamaica) 7" 1976
[7] 'Seven Letters' - Derrick Morgan
– Carib-Disc-Co (Jamaica)/Crab CR 08 & Jackpot JP 700 (UK) 7" 1969
[8] 'Give Me Some More Loving' – Slim Smith & The Uniques
– Afro (Jamaica)/Moodisc MU 3515 (UK) 7" 1971
[9] 'If I Did Know' – Roy Shirley – Afro (Jamaica)/Island WI 3125 (UK) 7" 1968
[10] 'Time Is The Master' – John Holt – Moodisc (Jamaica)/Cactus CTLP 109 (UK) LP 1973

he produced them but it's me. Some of the so called people up here put it out and said it was Mudies but they don't really know the story.

Plenty people me start you know... It was Christmas Eve and this guy came into the shop with this bag... like a travelling bag... over his shoulder and stood up there so I said *"Can I help you?"* And he said *"Me a look for Johnny Clarke"* and I said *"Johnny come and get him money and gone long time. Why? Are you a friend of Johnny Clarke's?"* And he said Johnny promised him something so I said *"Like what?"* and he said *"I want to go and buy a pair of shoes and a suit of clothes. Me and Johnny Clarke are friends you know"*. So I said *"Any friend of Johnny Clarke's is a friend of mine"* and then me say *"Alright I can do that"* so I sent him down Aunt Ive's shop. She was married to one of my friends who was a shoemaker at the time... he used to have a shoe factory in Waterhouse... my friend for years.

So I said *"Go in there, tell Aunt Ive to 'phone me and take any shoes you like. Then go down to Randy's..."* Keith who was Vincent Randy Chin's brother used to run a boutique... *"and take any clothes you want then call me and I will make sure you get it"*. So the guy went off about his business and I called Aunt Ive and said to give him the shoes and I called Keith and said *"Give him the things he wants"* and Keith said *"Like how much?"* and I said *"Give him anything and make a note of it and I'll take care of it"*. And I forgot all about him but then I saw him come back with his hand in his bag. I said *"Where's the things man? Didn't the people give them to you? Me and them talked on the 'phone"*.

He said *"Mr Lee I don't want nothing you know! Me is a man who was sent to come and shoot you but the way you were so nice... the way you dealt with me so good and you don't know me from nowhere"* and he took the gun out of his bag. *"See it there? And now the only thing I would like to do is spar[1] with a man like you Sir!"* and I said *"Well if you're going to spar with me you can't have the gun. You'll have to put that up"*. Then he said *"What are you doing tomorrow?"* and I said *"I'm going to the Christmas morning shows"*. He said *"Where do you live?"* and I said *"down Greenwich Farm"* and I gave him the address.

So Christmas morning he came and I said *"You're sure you don't have your gun?"* so he said *"No Mr Lee... I'm done with that"* and me and him jumped in the car and went up to about three stage shows at the Carib[2],

---

[1]spar: a friend (from sparring partner) so to *"spar with a man like you"* means to be your friend
[2] Carib Theatre, Cross Roads, Kingston 5

the State[1] and the Regal[2] Theatres. We just went from stage show to stage show and then I started him in the business as he said he wanted to try something. He was mixed up after that in the Green Bay Incident[3]... I haven't seen him from that.

I gave plenty of men a bligh[4] to start over with their life. People wanted to come to England but when they came up they started to give me pure problems. When charter flights first started to Jamaica I used to get free tickets and give them. When the plane used to come to Jamaica with the tourists it used to go back empty so I'd get customers for them to go to England. They'd sell so many and the rest of the tickets were mine. Sometimes I'd have ten tickets and I'd say *"Who wants to go to England tonight? I have ten tickets to leave here now"*. Some men jumped at the chance and because Immigration were expecting people who were just coming back from their holidays all they'd say was *"You had a nice time?"* and a man could come here get married and get his stay. Immigration was easier in those days... they'd just meet you on the tarmac... stamp your passport and say *"Have a nice holiday!"* Sometimes they'd say to Immigration *"We're just coming back from our holiday"* come to the country and never went back. Came for a holiday and just stayed. Some came back to Jamaica and some stayed. We still have a few of them around... you never needed visas or nothing. But some of the people started to mash it up and smuggle and a whole heap of things... they called down a disaster on us.

They started doing some way out things, man. In the music business from you start men just come from nowhere with *"Boy! You're the boss!"* and if you talk to a man and a man talk wrong to you they just took it over and beat them up. Sometimes me and a man would argue about something and they'd take it over and cut up the man and I started to get a bad reputation and people were afraid of me. They put themselves on your payroll and all them type of things.

A friend of mine came down the shop one morning and told me: *"Striker... last night I saw a gunman kill two men who were standing up beside me! It's a good thing I was your friend. The gunman killed two men and just stood up beside me and waved his gun at me and said 'You're still amongst Striker. You're alright'..."* And at the same time he was telling me the gunman came up on his motorbike and said *"Did you tell Striker about it?"* and I said *"The man hasn't*

---

[1] State Theatre, Old Hope Road, Cross Roads, Kingston 5
[2] Regal Theatre, Old Hope Road, Cross Roads, Kingston 5
[3] Green Bay Incident: five suspected gang members were shot dead on 5th January 1978 at a bay to the west of Kingston by what was alleged to be an Army firing squad. A further five were left for dead but they miraculously lived to recount the story
[4] bligh: helping hand/a favour

told me anything!" He said *"Through you and Striker are friends you're cool man... make him tell you about last night".* I said *"No!"* and he got on his big motorbike and rode off. Probably if my friend had said he had told me about it the gunman would have said *"He's talked!"* and they can't take no chances with a witness.

Another time Cornell Campbell came to me and said he'd just seen two men rob the Dairy Farmers place and so I said *"Cornell. That is none of our concern you know".* Then one of them came in the shop and I saw his gun in the waist of his pants. I said *"Cornell give me a minute and make I talk to this man".* He was going to shoot Cornell so I said to him *"Cornell don't know you man! Him only a talk. He don't tell. He doesn't know you're one of the men".* He said he was going to sit down in the shop so I said *"Spend as much time as you want"* and I had to convince the gunman. I went and spoke to Cornell and said *"Cornell. Next time when you see something **think** before you talk because that is one of the gunmen and he wanted to shoot you. Next time you see anything happen... be careful".* Then Cornell and him started talking and they became brethren and Cornell became **his** singer.

So I've seen a whole heap of things happen in this thing and that's why I did change and start to make some music named lover's rock and them old time soul records. The record business is like politics... different strokes for different folks. I can make any music! I start make music for mum and dad with Johnny Clarke and them people singing some old time Shirley & Lee tunes and make a market for myself with Tim Chandell[1] and Jackie Edwards... 'Come To Me Softly'[2]... and them kind of songs.

It was to get rid of them. I never came out of the business and I didn't really cool down... I eased up and did turn to making soul and rhythm & blues music because it got too tough. I don't know why they try and mix this music with gangsterism... it hold back the music more than anything. The music start to get too political... the drug barons start to come into it now and wash them money. So when the gunmen in Jamaica started coming amongst we and started doing things to hurt people I started making tunes with singers like Jackie Edwards. You never hear much about them 'pon the radio but they outsell the reggae thing. They said *"You're getting soft"* but they stopped coming round.

---

[1] Tim Chandell: UK based singer whose 'The Loving Moods Of' - Tim Chandell – Orbitone OLP 011 (UK) LP 1977 album proved very popular in the late Seventies

[2] 'Come To Me Softly' – Jimmy James – WIRL (Jamaica)/Dice CC15 (UK) 7" 1963. An early Lyndon Pottinger production that helped to set the template for the slow, sentimental ballad style favoured by the older generation that would later become known as big people's music

Cornell Campbell, 101 Orange Street

KEEL MUSIC
BMI
ZTSP 87364

VOCAL

Time 2:15

STICK BY ME (AND I'LL STICK BY YOU)
(Sheppard, Bassett, Baskerville)
SHEP AND THE
LIMELITES
45-H-757

HULL RECORDS, INC., NEW YORK CITY

ALL RIGHTS OF THE MANUFACTURER AND OF THE OWNER OF THE RECORDED WORK RESERVED UNAUTHORISED PUBLIC PERFORMANCE, BROADCASTING AND COPYING OF THIS

Stick By Me
JOHN HOLT

UPSETTER RECORDS

PRODUCED
AND DIRECTED
BY: LEE PERRY

DREAMLAND
(BUNNY)
THE WAILERS

MY DREAM ISLAND
(Al Johnson)
EL TEMPOS

45   45

[VJ]   [VJ]
VEE-JAY   VEE-JAY
RECORDS   RECORDS

PROMOTIONAL PROMOTIONAL
COPY   COPY

45   45

63-3341 — VOCAL
Conrad Pub.-BMI
Time: 2:37
VJ 580

TANKA

SOLDIER TAKE OVER
YELLOW MAN & FAT HEAD

J.T.

J - 107 - A
BMI

45 rpm
Prod. by

J. Nash
A. Jenkins
P. Khouri

Time: 2:30
Recorded in
Federal Record
Studios

HOLD ME TIGHT
(Johnny Nash)
JOHNNY NASH
Arr. and cond. by
Arthur Jenkins and Lyn Taitt

MANUFACTURED BY FEDERAL RECORD MFG. CO. LTD. JAMAICA.

152

Chapter 18 The Record Business... This Is Reggae Music

Old time people in Jamaica say *"Jackass says the world is not level"*[1]. Heh, heh, heh... that's the record business but sometimes you have to comment on it. You've got to see the little man and encourage him because the man who you run out of the studio one day it's tomorrow he has the big hit! So even if you didn't like his song stay with him and encourage him. I remember at the time when Buju[2] was starting I used to record Jackie Edwards and them because the deejay thing wasn't really my thing then so I carried him round to Jammys in his school uniform but Jammy never paid him no mind... then Buju came out of the box.

Yellowman[3] was called Yellowboy. He used to come round Joe Gibbs[4] at night time and they used to say *"Go back to the almshouse Yellowboy"* and they'd kick him around the place. Yellowman held the mic. and they took it and disinfected it and scorned it. I said to Ruddy Thomas[5]... who we used to call Flick... any time you get some money record Yellowman 'cause you did a tune with him named 'Government Boots Is Not Your Own'[6] for a guy named Tanka over the 'Lady Lady'/'Johnny'Dollar'[7] rhythm. Yellowman was up at Joe Gibbs' studio every night and they'd take liberties until one night I said *"Give*

---

[1] *"Jackass says the world is not level"*: a donkey finds it difficult to balance when it's on its back. The rest of the world, therefore, does not appear to be level from its vantage point. Not everyone understands the concept of fair play

[2] Buju Banton: Mark Anthony 'Buju Banton' Myrie one of Jamaica's most consistently inspired deejays of the Nineties and the New Millennium

[3] Yellowman: Winston 'Yellowman' Foster albino and international star. The most popular and biggest selling deejay of the Eighties

[4] Joe Gibbs Recording Studio, 24 Retirement Crescent, Kingston 5

[5] Ruddy Thomas: also known as Flick Wilson singer and recording engineer at Joe Gibbs' studio

[6] 'Soldier Take Over' – Yellowman & Fat Head – Taxi & Tanka (Jamaica) 7" 1981
one of Yellowman's first breakthrough records

[7] 'Lady Lady'/'Johnny Dollar': 'Johnny Dollar' - Roland Burrell – Taxi (Jamaica) 7" 1982

him a play of the rhythm there... " ET[1] will give you studio time and I said *"Just do it!"*

At that time Greensleeves[2] had just come and they talked to Jammy but Jammy said he had his own Yellowman! Jammy recorded a guy named Peter Yellow[3] who later became Purple Man and when he went back to Chris[4] he said *"No. We don't need this! We need this guy 'pon the cassette!"* And so they called Junjo[5] and Junjo caught Yellowman. Niney had recorded a whole heap of tune with Yellowman for Channel One but Jo Jo wouldn't put them out so Junjo and Greensleeves caught the next thing and Yellowman became a superstar... big overnight superstar like Bob Marley and thing!

And so the badness started running down and the next thing the liberties stop and they were dying to see him come through Joe Gibbs' gate. But Yellowman didn't bother to come there! Every night Junjo had him making LPs non stop and Yellowman put Junjo and Greensleeves on the map. Yet before Yellowman couldn't make it 'cause he was different. You understand? Yellowman became a superstar and although he used to live in an almshouse where poor people live he came out and got himself together and had a family and all that. Then he became King Yellow... and all the people who used to put disinfectant on his mic. would have liked to have two Yellowman from that time on their tape!

Like at first a Rastaman was a *"black heart man"*... you understand? The parents used to say keep away from those people because they smoke ganja and do this and that and now the Rastaman is at the forefront of everything! Bob Marley had Chris Blackwell behind him and I can't knock Chris. Chris promoted the music big in foreign[6] and then I started bringing artists to England so that everybody could get a fair share. I carried back money for Bob Marley and everybody so when I went back to Jamaica I'd just walk and issue cheques and that made me popular with the artists and everybody. So you have to start from the beginning. I used to make the people know... but they can't stop you from living because you have to live... it's not only the giants them. They used to have a saying *"it's the small dog keep the big dog going"* and some of the American singers the reggae bring them back!

---

[1] ET: Errol 'ET'/Errol T' Thompson
[2] Greensleeves: Greensleeves Records, 44 Uxbridge Road, Shepherds Bush, London W12 one of the leading UK reggae companies in the Eighties and Nineties
[3] Peter Yellow: also known as Purple Man. Another albino deejay
[4] Chris: Chris Cracknell head of A & R at Greensleeves Records
[5] Junjo: Henry 'Junjo' Lawes. Born 1960. Died 14th June 1999. One of the most important and successful record producers of the Eighties
[6] in foreign: overseas/international

Listen to 'Without You'[1] by Donnie Elbert and you a hear Donnie Elbert[2] sing some reggae. You ever hear that tune? Mrs King used to put out tunes for me too... Glen Adams and Roy Shirley sang that rhythm originally[3]. What we used to do is run off a copy and keep it and send the two track tapes to England so they could do their own mixes. Rita and Benny King did put Donnie Elbert on the rhythm in London (sings) *"Without you, without you..."* so 'Without You' was done up here and I carried it back to Jamaica and released it. Donnie Elbert is dead now.

Reggae brought back Johnny Nash with 'Hold Me Tight'[4]... Lyn Taitt did play it, you know. When it was first coming to England it was coming up on pre[5] but Federal wasn't putting it out fast enough and the people really wanted it so this man just cut it and started pirating it and selling 'Hold Me Tight' and 'Cupid' on white label... it wasn't on no label. Then Johnny Nash came to Jamaica and said *"Show me the man that put out the tune! I'd like to meet this guy"*. Instead of Johnny Nash being vexed with him he took his hand and gave him five hundred pounds and said *"Buy a drink! Thank you, man, for promoting me in England!"* Yeah! Him pirate the tune and Johnny Nash gave him five hundred pounds!

You had Clyde McPhatter come up here too! Just before he died he sang some tunes with Sydney Crooks[6] for Trojan[7]. You didn't know that?

---

[1] 'Without You' – Donnie Elbert (arranged by John Feddy) New Wave NW 001 (UK) 7" 1968
'Without You' – Donnie Elbert - Deram DM 235 (UK) 7" 1969
'Without You' – Donnie Elbert & The Pama All Stars - Unity (Jamaica) 1969
A Number One Jamaican hit
[2] Donnie Elbert: American rhythm & blues and soul singer who was always very popular in Jamaica. Born 25th May 1936. Died 26th January 1989
[3] 'Lonely Girl' – Glen Adams & Roy Shirley – Giant GN 33 (UK) 7" a 1968 rock steady update of 'Hey There Lonely Boy' - Ruby & The Romantics - Kapp (USA) 7" from 1963
[4] 'Hold Me Tight'/'Cupid' – Johnny Nash - Joda (Jamaica) 7" 1968. An important record with Texan born Johnny Nash backed by two beautiful Lyn Taitt rock steady rhythms which reached Number Five in the UK National Charts in August 1968 when it was eventually officially released on Regal Zonophone (RZ 3010). Produced at the Federal studios by Johnny Nash, Arthur Jenkins & Paul Khouri and arranged and conducted by Arthur Jenkins & Lyn Taitt. Johnny Nash has never been given the credit that his groundbreaking crossover success deserves. *"Then we also had a lot of involvement with foreign musicians coming down here like Johnny Nash with his entire band. He did a lot of sounds at Federal."* Paul Khouri
[5] pre: pre-release a Jamaican pressed seven inch record available only in specialist record shops and usually sold at twice or three times the price of a released single
[6] Sydney Crooks: of The Pioneers, who was also a record producer, was then resident in London
[7] *"He was in London around 1970/71... down on his luck."* Rob Bell quoted in 'Young, Gifted & Black'. Trojan released one single 'Denver'/'Tell Me' – Clyde McPhatter B&C 106 (UK) 7" 1970

And 'nough of them reggae tunes are foreign tunes... it's only when a tune hit big! But we never knew about publishing in those days. In our time we never had any publishing in Jamaica and on three quarters of the songs it says the copyright is controlled! They just gave it their own name... it's coming like the tune that Dawn Penn[1] did sing and the tune that Bunny Wailer sang 'Dreamland'[2]... originally 'My Dream Island'[3]. Most of these tunes... these things come to light. 'The Further You Look'[4] and look 'pon 'I Want A Love I Can See'[5] not 'Love I Can Feel'[6] originally by The Temptations. 'Thief In The Night' by Percy Sledge[7] John Holt called that 'Stealing, Stealing'[8] when he sung it for Treasure Isle and plenty people believe it's John Holt write it. You know 'You Don't Care'[9] is a Curtis Mayfield song too? It named 'You'll Want Me Back'[10]. So plenty of these Jamaican songs are cover versions but through they never had copyright law a man would just change the name and say it's him write it.

But most of these tunes a man claimed he did write... the people say they wrote it and when it comes to light they say they made a mistake and correct it. You understand? A man called me the other day about a tune that Ernest Wilson sang for me and said that he wrote it: *"Bunny you know that tune..."* (sings) *"I'm just a sentimental man..."*[11] Delroy changed the words when he did (sings) *"I'm in a dancing mood"*[12] and 'Close To Me'[13]... Delroy just took out parts of it. He never sung the whole song but the others sang the right words.

---

[1] 'You Don't Love Me' – Dawn Penn – Coxsone (Jamaica)/Studio One SO 2030 (UK) 1967 & 'You Don't Love Me (No No No)' – Dawn Penn – Steely & Clevie (Jamaica)/Big Beat A 8295 (UK) 7" 1994 originally 'No, No, No' – Willie Cobbs – Mojo (USA) 7" 1960

[2] 'Dreamland' – The Wailers – Upsetter (Jamaica & UK US 371) 7" 1970

[3] 'My Dream Island' - El Tempos – Vee Jay (USA) 7" 1963

[4] 'The Further You Look' – John Holt – Federal (Jamaica)/Horse HOSS 22 (UK) 7" 1972 originally 'The Further You Look The Less You See' – The Temptations – Gordy (USA) 7" 1963

[5] 'I Want A Love I Can See' – The Temptations – Gordy (USA) 7" 1963

[6] 'A Love I Can Feel' – John Holt – Coxsone (Jamaica)/Bamboo BAM 44 (UK) 7" 1971

[7] 'Thief In The Night' – Percy Sledge – Atlantic (USA) 7" 1971

[8] 'Stealing' – John Holt – Treasure Isle (Jamaica)/Duke DU 73 (UK) 7" 1970

[9] 'You Don't Care' – The Techniques – Treasure Isle (Jamaica & UK TI 7001) 7" 1967

[10] 'You'll Want Me Back' – The Impressions – ABC Paramount (USA) 7" 1963

[11] 'Sentimental Man' - Ernest Wilson – Crab CR 45 (UK) 7" 1970 originally 'Sentimental Man' – The Unifics – Kapp (USA) 7" 1968

[12] 'Dancing Mood' – Delroy Wilson – All Stars (Jamaica)/Island WI 3013 (UK) 7" 1966 originally 'Dancing Mood' – The Tams – 'Presenting The Tams' - ABC Paramount (USA) LP 1964

[13] 'Close To Me' – Delroy Wilson – Coxsone (Jamaica)/Island WI 3039 (UK) 7" 1966 originally 'Close To Me' – The Tams - 'Presenting The Tams' - ABC Paramount (USA) LP 1964

Shelly did start as Count Shelly[1] before Third World and there was a mishap with one of those foreign tunes that Mudies gave him to release. Mudies did a tune with Dennis Walks and changed the name over to 'Margaret'[2] but it was an old rhythm & blues tune with Marvin & Johnny (sings) *"Oh sugar"*[3]... Dennis Walks didn't write the tune! They changed one word of it... changed 'sugar' to 'Margaret'. Get the original one, man, and play it! 'Nough foreign tunes...

Count Shelly... he's a character you know... my good friend. When I came up here first Shelly had his sound system Count Shelly from the North. He used to rule Stoke Newington way. Shelly started putting out records but the records that he was putting out were pirated so I said *"Shelly. You look like Duke Reid but you can't do that! Here's some tunes... you can pre-release them[4]..."* I was buying a house in Jamaica and at the time Trojan did just sell out to Saga[5]. Count said *"Give me them man"* and the next thing I know Count pre-released them and before I went back to Jamaica he gave me £10,000 in my hand! I was shocked 'cause since I came into the business I never get so much money yet! So I said *"Count it's better me and you work... put out the tunes... release them!"* So I stopped doing business with Trojan for quite a while... that time Pama was out of the business. They were just starting back when Shelly got in.

Away from Island Shelly was the Number One up here in the Bob Marley era... 'cause here comes Johnny Clarke taking over the scene from Dennis Brown. So Cornell Campbell and Johnny Clarke ruled the airwaves and Shelly got all those to release in England. He started to put out King Tubbys dub and Shelly did get very big. He set up World Enterprise and Third World Records[6]. He was going on good man! Then Shelly leave and go to America and started working with Jammy when he became King Jammy. He got a good run and... for one man... he did really well. Sid Bucknor did bring the Third World label from Jamaica but through Siddy was too slow Shelly just continue and Siddy got left behind. You can't take a year to put out a tune!

---

[1] Count Shelly: Ephraim 'Count Shelly' Barrett London based sound system operator, record shop proprietor/distributor (Third World, Body Music & World Enterprise) and record producer who also licensed Jamaican records for UK release on a variety of labels including Count Shelly, Live & Love, Paradise & Third World
[2] 'Margaret' – Dennis Walks – HAM (Jamaica)/Count Shelly CS 055 (UK) 7" 1974
[3] 'Sugar' – Marvin & Johnny – Modern (USA) 78rpm 10" 1954 and also 'Margaret' – The Royal Holidays – Penthouse (USA)/London 45 HLU 8722 (UK) 7" 1958
[4] pre-release them: sell the records at a higher price before officially releasing them
[5] Trojan Records was sold to Marcel Rodd's Saga Records in 1975
[6] World Enterprise and Third World Records: Count Shelly's shops and distribution in New York and London

It come like Derrick Morgan and Prince Buster with 'They Got To Come' and 'Forward March' with Harry J's 'Liquidator' when The Staple Singers did 'I'll Take You There'[1]. They disputed that all the while. 'Liquidator' is close to 'Girl I Got A Date'[2]... near to it. You see if I like 'Girl I Got A Date' and I used a couple of bars you wouldn't recognise it because I'd put a swinging bridge in the tune. Make the bass player go right back inna that then solo then bridge again and come back so when you hear it it's a totally different tune. Or you make the bass player play it back ways so you create a new sound. With 'Bongo Natty' that Owen Gray sung for me it was like 'Girl I've Got A Date' with a different intro and it sound like so.

Then they copied 'None Shall Escape The Judgement'[3]. Yeah man... 'cause we didn't know nothing about publishing at that time so Larry Sevitt[4] and a guy named Tony Seddon[5] dealt with it. When 'Egyptian Reggae'[6] came out the bass line was Chinna's and the other part belongs to Family Man. He played guitar on that session... where the change is *"Arise black man"*... that's Family Man. It was giving them trouble so him and Chinna worked out the chords and that was it. And Chinna played a brilliant solo... something like Santana[7]... it kind a introduced guitar solos into reggae. You understand? So when these people copied the tune Larry and them had to fight it 'cause Larry was my good friend. I think Johnny Clarke did register it at one time but they said no. If anybody it's Earl Zero and Chinna Smith... you only sing it so you can't do that... you might get a percentage of part of it but you can't register the tune. So I did clear up that so everybody got a piece of the action. I think I did get a piece of the action

---

[1] 'I'll Take You There' – The Staple Singers – Stax (USA & 2025 110 UK) 7" 1972 An Al Bell production for Stax Records, Memphis that allegedly used the introduction and rhythm to 'Liquidator' – Harry J All Stars – Harry J (Jamaica & UK TR 675) 7" which reached Number Nine in the UK National Charts in the autumn of 1969. The rhythm for 'Liquidator' was based around the bass line to 'Girl I Have Got A Date' by Alton Ellis *"...Island owner Chris Blackwell had given Jimmy Johnson a paid vacation in Jamaica. Johnson took some time to visit local recording studios and record stores, picking up a slew of current Jamaican records along the way. Upon his return he distributed the records to all the members of the Muscle Shoals rhythm section... In actuality the record's introduction, bass line, and general groove were lifted directly from a 1969 Jamaican instrumental recording by The Harry J All Stars entitled 'The Liquidator'... this was probably one of the records Jimmy Johnson had brought back from Jamaica..."*
Rob Bowman: Soulsville U.S.A. The Story of Stax Records
[2] 'I Have Got A Date' –Alton Ellis – Dutchess (Jamaica)/Doctor Bird DB 1059 (UK) 7" 1968
[3] 'None Shall Escape The Judgement' – Johnny Clarke
– Justice (Jamaica)/Explosion EX 2089 (UK) 7" 1974
[4] Larry Sevitt: Jamaica Sounds label
[5] Tony Seddon: *"Tony Seddon used to be Trojan's lawyer at the time..."* Bunny 'Striker' Lee
[6] 'Egyptian Reggae' – Jonathan Richman & The Modern Lovers – Beserkley BZZ 2 (UK) 7" 1977 A Number Five UK hit
[7] Santana: rock band featuring Mexican American guitarist Carlos Santana

as the producer and the man who spent the money to make the rhythm and everything like that.

You don't want to watch what the Joneses are doing... you can't try keep up with the Joneses or you're going to fall flat. But the business can reverse on you sometimes. Years later Gladdy played on a session for me one day upstairs at Sonic Sounds studio[1] and the young musicians a laugh after him and I said *"No. You have to take time. The whole a we never young! That man is Gladstone Anderson and him get old but he was one of the first men who played on my sessions with Lyn Taitt. He helped me stay in the business until now. Make him play and if he can't get it we'll call the session a day!"* He sat down and he got it. It was just because he seemed like an old man... yet he used to arrange at Treasure Isle and everywhere! But when the time come when you're not as young as you used to be you can still **feel.** You're young at heart still.

It's like if you have a set of children it's better you just love every one of them 'cause if you show this one love more than another one then they're going to get vexed with you. Some kids carry it all till you get old and they say *"Boy he's your favourite son. You never used to treat me good but you used to treat that one so..."* so you try to do it 'pon an equal basis the best you can.

I'll say it again... every man is a man and every man is a star in his own right and their day will come. You've got to show love to everyone.

---

[1] Sonic Sounds: Sonic Sounds Record Manufacturing Co. Ltd., 25 Retirement Road, Kingston 5

Bunny 'Striker' Lee, Third World Records, London

Bunny 'Striker' Lee in the Tape Vaults

Chapter 19 National Honour And Award Version[1]

I stopped in America and I got a gold suit and a top hat from up here in London… it was well dignified. Everybody was talking about it. They put it on the front page in the paper saying this man Bunny Lee was the most dapper man in the ceremony. The suit was outstanding! They said the award was overdue and all that… it was a good feeling too because I'd got awards all over the world. They should have kept the ceremony where I collected my award at King's House but through it was raining they kept it at the indoor sports centre. A nice place for it too! They keep all the Reggae Academy Awards there. I heard Usain Bolt[2] got his on Monday too but he got a different one… the people in Jamaica a bawl but I said he deserved it! He is the youngest one to ever get it but I think the Prime Minister did the right thing. He should have got the Order of Merit… it's the next big one but a whole heap of people a bawl! Politics, politics too much politics…

---

[1] The Order of Distinction was conferred on Bunny 'Striker' Lee by the Jamaican Government in the autumn of 2008 for more than forty years of dedicated service to the music industry. It was one of the few subjects that he was uncharacteristically reticent to talk about and, instead, the report from *The Sunday Gleaner* tells the story

[2] Usain Bolt: the fastest sprinter in the world, and winner of three gold medals at the 2008 Olympic Games, Usain Bolt was awarded the Order of Distinction later that year

The Sunday Gleaner, Kingston, Jamaica, 26th October 2008
'Striker' Gets His Due
Sadeke Brooks
Staff Reporter

Legendary record producer Edward O'Sullivan Bunny 'Striker' Lee has finally received the type of honour he was waiting for from his country. At last Monday's National Honours and Awards Ceremony at King's House 67 year old Lee was given the Order of Distinction in the rank of Officer for more than forty years of dedicated service to the music industry.

Other awardees at the ceremony who have been involved in the music industry were Thomas 'Tommy' Cowan, Joel Augustus 'Joe Gibbs' Gibson (deceased) and Cedella Marley-Booker (deceased) the mother of Bob Marley.

Lee said he was grateful because he had been waiting for an award of this nature from his country for years.

Apollo Award

"It's been a hard struggle but they gave me an award the other day and I am pleased. I even got the Apollo Award and people always ask me how I don't get anything from my own country but nothing ever happen before the time. This puts the icing on the cake" Lee told The Sunday Gleaner.

"When you get something from the Government... it took me forty odd years... but it finally came. I see people that we teach get recognition before us." Lee said.

Lee said he was happy to receive what had been due to him for years, but there are many other people who deserve awards but are sometimes forgotten. "You still have Owen Gray, Lee Perry, Derrick Harriott and many others. They are people that did a lot of work for the music 'cause they carried the music. It's not Bob Marley alone do it; it was teamwork." he said.

Lee is from a humble Kingston beginning. His father was a shoemaker and his mother was a housewife. Though the finances were limited Lee said he was taught to work hard and be satisfied with the little he had. With this drive, Lee began working at an early age. He worked at Uni Motors, Kingston Industrial Garage and even the Gleaner Company during his holidays before moving on to the music industry.

In the early Sixties Lee collected records from other producers like Duke Reid, Clement 'Coxsone' Dodd and Leslie Kong. He took these records to the Teenage Dance Party on JBC TV, on which he was a dancer, helping to promote many songs. He also had his own 'Bunny Lee Show' on JBC TV and RJR where he played music.

In 1968 Lee took his passion for music to England. However, the radio stations were not very receptive of this relatively new genre. There Lee helped to start Palmer Brothers (Pama) and Trojan Records with which he licensed his productions. "When I bring reggae to BBC them throw it in the rubbish bin. Is a station in England name Radio Caroline, which used to be out in the sea, that break the music. They used to come on in the evening and go right back into morning" he said. After that he went on to promote Jamaican music in Canada and the United States.

He was one of the pioneers of reggae, ska, dub, dancehall (toasting) and even a relatively unknown version of the music called 'John Crow Skank' which is a slower version of rock steady. "We is the trendsetter. We start dancehall," Lee said while noting the work that others like 'Coxsone' Dodd and Lee 'Scratch' Perry have done for Jamaican music. Lee said he has helped to make the music what it is today.

"From I come in the music it change 'cause I say every spoil is a style. Anything a man do I say make it stay. Even if the engineer want change it I say no. Make it stay," he told The Sunday Gleaner. "Barbara Lynn's 'If You Should Lose Me'… mistake in a it but it still go through and become a hit and a classic." However, he did not only allow mistakes to slide for experimental purposes. Sometimes, Lee said, he could not afford to pay the musicians so he simply had to make minor adjustments to old rhythms and make them relatively new.

Lee has worked with some of Jamaica's greatest musicians and singers. He worked on Slim Smith's 'Everybody Needs Love' (1969), Pat Kelly's 'How Long' (1970), Delroy Wilson's 'Better Must Come' (1971) which became a hit for UB40, Eric Donaldson's 'Cherry Oh Baby' (1971) and John Holt's 'Stick By

Me' (1971). He has also worked with The Mighty Diamonds, Bob Marley, Gregory Isaacs, Glen Adams, Roy Shirley, Dawn Penn, Derrick Morgan, The Uniques, Linval Thompson, Leroy Smart, Barry Brown, Joe Gibbs, Dennis AlCapone, U Roy, I Roy, Prince Jazzbo, U Brown, Dr Alimantado, Jah Stitch, Trinity, Tappa Zukie and Beenie Man when the dancehall 'doctor' was only ten years old.

Lee has had a long life in the music and he wants to do a book about it all...[1]

---

[1] He has now. Here it is...

Edward O'Sullivan Bunny 'Striker' Lee Order of Distinction in the rank of Officer 26th October 2008

Jamaica

Office of the Prime Minister

Jamaica House
Kingston

25th July 2008

Dear Mr Lee,

It gives me great pleasure to inform you that acting on my advice, His Excellency The Governor-General has conferred the honour of the Order of Distinction, in the rank of Officer (OD) upon you, in recognition of your over forty years of dedicated service to the Music Industry.

Your appointment to the Order, which takes effect on Independence Day, Wednesday, 6th August 2008, will be announced in the media on that date. Until the first public announcement you should treat this information as confidential.

The Ceremony of Investiture will be held at King's House on National Heroes Day, Monday, 20th October 2008.

It would, in the meantime, be appreciated if you would confirm your acceptance of this award by contacting the Secretary-General of the Orders of the Societies of Honour by telephone at 946-2268, 927-9941-3 or by facsimile at 927-9321.

Please accept my warm personal congratulations on your well-deserved honour.

Yours sincerely,

Bruce Golding
Prime Minister

Edward O'Sullivan Bunny 'Striker' Lee Order of Distinction in the rank of Officer 25th July 2008

Bunny 'Striker' Lee

Annette Wong Lee, Bruce Golding and Bunny 'Striker' Lee

Bunny 'Striker' Lee

Newton Williams, Caroline Robertson, Niney The Observer, Bunny 'Striker' Lee,
Asher, Portia Simpson Miller and Patrizia 'Trish' De Rosa

Annette Wong Lee, Bunny 'Striker' Lee and Portia Simpson Miller

Bunny 'Striker' Lee, Orlando Sinclair and Winston 'Merritone' Blake

Niney The Observer, Bunny 'Striker' Lee, Catherine James, Tappa Zukie and Aloun Assamba

Little Striker Lee, Dane Lee and Bunny 'Striker' Lee

Little Striker Lee, Bonnie Lee, Annette Wong Lee, Tonian Lee, Kirk Lee and Bunny 'Striker' Lee

Striker Strikes Again... Twenty Two Hits From Bunny 'Striker' Lee
Rock Steady 1967 to 1968

Music Field - Roy Shirley 1967

Duke Reid was so pleased with what I'd done with 'Baba Boom' that he gave me the studio time. The song won the Festival Song Competition because Desmond Dekker should have won and 'Baba Boom' won and that was when I left KIG. I only had twenty pounds to give to Lyn Taitt and he got a four piece band... himself and three others... and we did 'Music Field' with Roy Shirley. My brother, Don Lee, was working at WIRL as sales manager and he went to Mr Rae, Bunny Rae, an old army man. He always gave the little man a chance and Mr Rae took 'Music Field' and put it out. It came out on Lee... I made a label named Lee first.

My Conversation - Slim Smith & The Uniques 1968

Winston Grennan played the piano on 'My Conversation'. He played the drum on the rhythm track because after Lyn Taitt I started to work with Bobby Aitken & The Carib Beats. Winston Grennan was the drummer with the *"ding a ling"* piano on the voice track... it's even been versioned more than 'Never Let Go'. You know the two most versioned songs in the whole reggae business? 'My Conversation' with Slim Smith and the tune they call 'I'll Never Let You Go' with Slim Smith. Every singer that you can think of has a piece of 'My Conversation'.

The Russians Are Coming - Val Bennett 1968

We did over 'Take Five' and we were going to do it in the jazz form but I said *"No man. Make we rock it! Any tune can rock"* and Bobby Aitken and the bass went *"boom, boom, boom"* and slowed it right down. Winston Grennan was the drummer and we tried it. One cut! There was a comedy film called 'The Russians Are Coming' that was popular at the time and when 'The Russians Are Coming' came out it changed the whole business. It brought back instrumentals because everyone had stopped using wind instruments in the rock steady.

Early Reggae 1968 to 1969

Wet Dream - Max Romeo 1968

'Wet Dream' was a tune now! I put it on the 'Hold You Jack' rhythm. I asked Pat Kelly and all those man to voice it and they said *"No. We nah go voice that slack tune..."* All the big names at the time... nobody wanted to sing it and Maxie was the last man now. Maxie used to sing for Ken Lack with The Emotions but at that time he wasn't singing... he was working for me as a salesman. He said *"Boy... Striker I don't want to sing it"* and I said *"If you don't sing this tune then don't come to work tomorrow!"* Next thing Pama called me one day and said that me and Maxie Romeo have to come to England. The record spent twenty six weeks in the British chart and any time after that if I told a singer what to do then they had to do it! All the big singers... Pat Kelly, Slim Smith started that they'd never done shows in England... the least of the apostles... the underdog... was the first man to go in the British charts. A big thing! From ''Wet Dream' you don't know what's going to hit...

Bangarang - Lester Sterling & Stranger Cole 1968

Rock steady never had the organ shuffle. On a rock steady tune a horn man just played an intro, a solo and a little fill in. 'Bangarang' was the first reggae tune... it had the shuffle right through. It was a foreign tune. A jazz tune named 'Bongo Chant' but the guys were young as musicians and they couldn't hold the chords to the bridge. So I said to Lester Sterling *"make it into a two chord tune"* and Lester said *"How 'Bangarang' sound to you?"* and I said *"Make we try it now... (sings) Woman no want bangarang"...* it's just a take off from 'Bongo Chant'. It kind a come like an original tune added to the other part of Kenny's tune so it ended up it different. When it came out on the road it was the biggest tune for 1968 in Jamaica.

How Long - Pat Kelly 1969

Pat Kelly is one of the greatest singers ever. He was a very cool youth... the first time I recorded Pat Kelly was 'Somebody's Baby'[1] and 'Twelfth Of Never'[2]. We did it live with Bobby Aitken and his band at West Indies Records Limited in 1967. Pat Kelly was born in August like me... Pat Kelly will sit down here the whole day and don't say six words and you don't know what a man like that is thinking some times. But he's alright! He and I get on good... Pat Kelly, Slim Smith, Jackie Edwards, Owen Gray, everybody can sing... you name them. Pat Kelly's tune at the time was 'How Long'... he made other hits but he never made a tune bigger than 'How Long'.

One Thousand Tons Of Megaton - Roland Alphonso 1969

One of Roland Alphonso's biggest tunes was the version to 'Everybody Needs Love'... 'One Thousand Tons Of Megaton'. Roland played alto sax and Derrick Morgan deejayed 'pon it. If you listen to it you can hear Derrick make a mistake... Sylvan Morris wanted to stop the tape *"Cool it man!"* and I said *"No. Make it stay..."* He was doing it the same time as Roland was blowing and Family Man was playing one of Coxsone's organs. If you stopped everybody had to stop in those days! Then everybody would have to start over... I said *"Morris make it run with the mistake..."* Roland was cooking and you could feel the horns so we just made it go on and put it out same way. When it came out it was a runaway hit and Roland couldn't believe that the record had his name on it... himself as a solo artist.

---

[1] 'Somebody's Baby' - Pat Kelly – Lee's (Jamaica)/Island WI 3121 (UK) 7" 1968
[2] 'Twelfth Of Never' – Pat Kelly – Lee's (Jamaica)/Island WI 3124 (UK) 7" 1968

Reggae 1970 to 1972

Mr Chatterbox - Bob Marley 1970

Even to this day me and Niney have our ups and downs… you
understand? That's how 'Mr Chatterbox' came out … through
Niney. Bob and Bunny Wailer had done a tune already for
Coxsone named 'Mr Talkative' so at the start of the 'Mr
Chatterbox' record I said *"Bob so how the session work out?"*
and me and Bob a talk and me say *"Niney a come"* and Bob said
"him Mr Talkative that…" When you record Bob… in those days you mostly
have to do live recording with the band and the singers singing one time… if
Bob made a mistake and him start from the top again him sing something
different! He used to just make the songs up out of his head… and afterwards
he'd go back and learn it… Toots… Derrick Morgan… John Holt… they all
used to do it.

Stick By Me - John Holt 1971

John Holt is the seventh man that sang 'Stick By Me'. That was
the first tune voiced at Harry J's studio. When a studio opened
in Jamaica and they wanted to test it out they always send for
me so I'd always travel with a two track version of the tape.
John Holt and myself was driving… I said *"John… voice this
tune"* and John go round and voiced his version of the tune.
Delroy Wilson was the first man that did it but through I'd put it on a Byron Lee
LP[1] I couldn't put it out… and then Dennis Brown. That's why Dennis Brown
called Delroy Wilson teacher… Delroy showed the young Dennis Brown all the
phrases and all that. But Dennis was working with Derrick Harriott at the time
so it couldn't go out. Derrick was my friend and he said *"Mr Lee. We worked
hard to break the little artist there. You can't put it out and take him away so
early"* so I never put it out. Dennis was very upset when the tune came out with
John Holt. Then David Isaacs have a version, Cornell Campbell have a version,
Max Romeo have a version, The Cables have a version… a lot of people have a
version.

When I did 'Cherry Oh Baby' a guy called Huey Meaux[2] sent for me. I did a
tune with Jackie Edwards… 'Julie On My Mind'[3]… and they wanted Jackie so

---

[1] 'Stick By Me' - 'Better Must Come' – Delroy Wilson
– Dynamic Sounds (Jamaica) 1971/Trojan TRLS 44 (UK) LP 1972
[2] Huey P Meaux: American record producer based in Texas
[3] 'Julie On My Mind' – Jackie Edwards – Island WIP 602 (UK) 7" 1968

they asked me to come over to Texas. This guy used to do a lot of big artists... Freddy Fender[1] and all that. You know that Freddy Fender sang on one of my rhythms... 'Just Out Of Reach'... the one that John Holt sings. You never hear that? It was on an album (sings) *"Just out of reach..."* where he's riding a cow on the cover![2] They were trying to blend the soul and the reggae together. So I went to Texas and he asked me to bring some of the tunes that I'd done. And as him hear 'Stick By Me' he said *"This guy's singing flat... but this tune is going to be a hit! Who wrote the tune?"* and I said *"It's a Shep & The Limelites tune.[3] Why you say so Mr Meaux?"* He said any tune you can wake up shaving and hum it and sing it when you've heard it once then it's a hit... (sings) *"Stick by me... I'll stick by you..."* So I came back to Jamaica and just dropped the tune. I have the record now for the longest selling Number One in Jamaica with John Holt. It was the biggest tune in Jamaica for that year... John Holt's biggest local hit. Yeah.

Cherry Oh Baby - Eric Donaldson 1971

Well... one night the Festival eliminations were on and I went along with Delroy Wilson and some of the other artists. When this guy... Eric Donaldson... sung the tune Delroy bring him to me and I decided to record it the next day. At that time I was producing things for Dynamic and we did it in a studio that Byron Lee fixed up for me and Lloyd Charmers but they didn't like the sound. It had a different sound... I went back in and brought in Denzil Laing and the band that I used was an outside band with my drummer Lloyd Adams who we called 'Tin Leg'. That band was The Inner Circle and later half of it became Third World.

---

[1] Freddy Fender: Texan singer songwriter Born Baldemar Garza Huerta 4th June 1937. Died 14th October 2006. Baldemar changed his name to Freddy Fender in 1958: Fender from the guitar and Freddy because *"it would sell better with gringos"*

[2] 'Rock 'n' Country' – Freddy Fender – Dot (USA) LP 1976 The cover picture is actually an illustration of Freddy riding a bull, rodeo style, with his guitar strapped across his back

[3] 'Stick By Me (And I'll Stick By You)' – Shep & The Limelites – Hull (USA) 7" 1963 but originally released on an album from the previous year 'Our Anniversary' - Shep & The Limelites - Hull LP 1001 (USA) 1962

Better Must Come - Delroy Wilson 1971

In 1971 when Michael Manley was campaigning the PNP used my tune 'Better Must Come' by Delroy Wilson and Maxie Romeo's 'Let The Power Fall On I'... but Derrick Morgan did produce that... and the music reached the people and won the election. That was their manifesto... better must come. The music would speak for itself with all the artists of the time on the Bandwagon. So you find in every era if you have a good tune a politician will take it up...

Play It Cool - Alton Ellis 1972

Alton Ellis was a great artist too... Alton was alright... a good man. He's a singer who takes a little longer because he's a professional... a perfectionist right? Alton used to be a senior man at Duke Reid and then he went on tour with Coxsone[1]. Alton Ellis and his sister Hortense! 'Play It Cool' was a tune now that was voiced at Dynamics. There was another guy doing the session but him did run out of money and through I was in charge of the studio I said... we used to call Alton Two Smart because he was more than smart enough to outsmart one man... *"Two Smart. Make we finish the tune and me and the guy will talk some business..."* so we voiced it. You can hear his sister Hortense (sings) *"Rock you, rock you, rock rock on time..."* So when we'd voiced 'Rock On Time' now... the guy who did make the rhythm... we said *"Alright. What do you want to do? Put out the tune or do you want me to put it out?"* He said *"Look Mr Lee. Sell it... just take it and give me back the money that you make"* and I did give Alton a cut to put 'pon him LP[2] and I had it for quite a while before I put it out. It should be named 'Rock On Time' but through Alton sang 'Play It Cool' we just called it 'Play It Cool'.

---

[1] The Soul Vendors 1967 UK Tour featured vocalists Ken Boothe & Alton Ellis
[2] 'Still In Love' – Alton Ellis – Horse HRLP 708 (UK) LP 1977

Roots, Rockers And Flying Cymbals 1973 to 1975

God Helps The Man - Leroy Smart 1973

That is one of his first songs. It's two times I do it with him
you know. I did it down at West Indies Records Ltd first
(sings) *"God helps the man that helps himself..."* It was the
first tune I did with Leroy Smart but he did some other tunes
for himself...

You Are My Angel - Horace Andy 1974

Earl 'Wire' Lindo from The Wailers arranged the bass line and
everything down at Harry J's studio. That was the first time I
recorded Horace Andy... his first tune for me. I give Earl
'Wire' Lindo a lot of credit for that arrangement... he used to
arrange plenty of my tunes you know... and as I said... The
Wailers band were The Aggrovators before. But every musician
who comes to my sessions... whether you work or not you get paid...'cause I
invited you.

None Shall Escape The Judgement - Johnny Clarke 1974

This tune now... I was going home one night and I heard
Chinna and Earl Zero playing this tune and Earl Zero was
singing *"None shall escape the judgement in this time... Arise
black man... Jahoviah has come forward into Babylon... To
declare equal rights and justice among the heathens... I love
and I serve him..."* I come and I listened and I said *"I like the
tune, you know, Chinna"* and Earl Zero said *"Mr Lee. Come tomorrow down to
Duke Reid's studio. I think I'm going to record it"*. They had *"Dum, dum,
dum... dum dum dum...dum dum dum dum dum dum dum"* and the beat of it. So
the next day we met at Duke's studio. I put in the other part... the change part...
because the song was too short *"As I approach the gates of Zion I can hear the
choir singing..."* all of them things there is me.

So I asked Johnny Clarke to sing it with Earl Zero ... they rehearsed it the
whole day... but Earl Zero could only sing the front part so that night I asked
Siddy[1] to run off a cut of the rhythm... *"I a go try something"*. That night me

---

[1] Siddy: Sidney Bucknor

and Johnny Clarke... we were always around together... we were up at Tubbys and Tubbys said *"This guy can't manage the song"* and I said *"Johnny. Do you think you could a do it?"* and Johnny went into Tubby's studio. One cut! One cut! No error or nothing... 'cause he'd been rehearsing it with Earl Zero the whole day.

I used to love eat the chicken wings and I'd said *"Santa... that drum sound on 'Here I Am Baby'... I like it"* so when the rhythm done I said *"It's named flyers"* through the chicken wings. Sly had played it[1] but he never realised what he had and because I loved my chicken wings we just named it flyers (sings) *"tsk, tsk, tsk, tsk..."* So that night when we went up to Tubbys with the rhythm I said *"Tubbs. You'll like this rhythm... it's different. When we do it I want something like it's from outer space on the intro"*. Tubbys passed it through the high pass filter on his machine where he pushed up one of the things on his board and it thinned it out. Styled it out man! (sings) *"tsk, tsk, tsk..."* I named it flyers but they didn't know what flyers was!

So Tubbys had it on the sound system for a while and the people them forced me to release it. I did leave and go to England and I was going to give it to Delroy Wilson. I bring it for Delroy to sing it and Delroy said *"Striker... the youth sing it good! Give the youth a break man. Let the youth sing it... if you want I will sing it but I figure you should give the youth a bligh[2]."* So I said *"Alright Delroy. If you say so..."* That time Delroy was in England so we didn't bother voice it. We voiced some other tune...

So when we went back to Jamaica I said to Johnny Clarke *"You have to like Delroy Wilson because I was going to make him sing over the tune in England"*. Tapper Zukie came to me and said *"Striker? You have a tune there on Tubbys sound. It a mad! Every time it plays the dance catch a fire"*. I said *"Which tune?"* so Tapper told me *"the tune that the new youth a sing... Studio Idler"*. Studio Idler is what we used to call Johnny Clarke because he was always around the studio.

Then Phillip Smart come and he said *"Boy Mr Lee... I'm tired of cutting dubs of this tune. You have to put out the tune"* so I said to Phillip *"Take a mix of off this tune..."* so when Phillip was mixing it Tubbys a fly in and said *"What's happening? I've cut 'nough dub with people and you can't put out this now because the dub people will come back..."* so I said *"Tubbs we're mixing this*

---

[1] 'It's A Shame' – Delroy Wilson – Well Charge (Jamaica) 7" 1975 and 'Here I Am Baby Come And Take Me' – Al Brown & Skin, Flesh & Bones Inc – Tit For Tat (Jamaica)/Trojan TR 7935 (UK) 7" 1973
[2] bligh: helping hand/favour

tune to go send to England for Fatman. We're not going to put it out" and Tapper and Tubbys started to quarrel. Tapper said to Tubbys *"Let the new tune go out on the road"* and Tubbys said *"No man!"* So I didn't bother row. We just took a rough cut of the master and mixed the version. Tubbs said *"Where are you sending the version? I'll send it..."* and I said *"No. I have somebody going to England this evening and by the time you mix it yourself and send it they'll be gone. It's just Fatman's sound it's for"*. So at the same time I just went down to Federal to master it with the version and everything and when the tune came out it had the *"swwwt, swwwt, swwwt..."* Phillip Smart mixed the first version that went out on the road... not Tubbys[1]!

And Tubbys was vexed... but everybody started flocking to Tubbys then and I said *"It's better you put out the tune because now everybody wants different dub cuts"*. Sound men started to line up at Tubbys' gate for different pieces and different cuts with their sound's name in it and things. So it was a feather in his cap... but he didn't want it released! But from Tubbs put out that tune there was no turning back 'cause **every** tune we put out we put the rhythm behind it. But flyers is not the right name really and everybody started to get puzzled when Johnny Clarke hit with this flyers now.

A Dance In A Greenwich Farm - Cornell Campbell 1975

That was a rhythm that I made when I was making an LP with John Holt... a flyers LP 'cause John always wanted that type of thing... and someone called to say 'Help Me Make It Through The Night'[2] with Tony Ashfield hit in England and he had to leave to come and do 'Top Of The Pops'. So when him leave now he leave the rhythm and the plan was for him to voice it when he come back.

So we go a Tubbys... Tubbys had a contest that night... him a play at Greenwich Farm and I passed and see the dance full. So I see some guys up there and I said *"Cornell! The tune that John Holt was going to sing 'pon it. You know the Bobby Day tune?* (sings) *'Well I went to a dance the other night and everybody was there... over and over and over'"*[3] and this idea hit me so I said *"Cornell. Write this tune here...* (sings) *'Well I went to a dance in Greenwich Farm King Tubbys and the dreads were there... there was dread,*

---

[1] 'This A The Best Version' – The Aggrovators – Justice (Jamaica) 7" 1974
[2] 'Help Me Make It Through The Night' – John Holt – Trojan TR7909 (7") 1974
A Number Six UK hit
[3] 'Over And Over' – Bobby Day – Class (USA)/London 45 HL 8726 (UK) 7" 1958

dread, dread and dread and natty roots everywhere'" I finished write it and Chinna sing harmony. *"But when I man take a stop it was just a baldhead informer just a try a thing..."* Right? But the dread them come back to the dance and dub to King Tubby's beat. That was one of the first sound system specials that go 'pon the road. 'Cause by the Monday morning I had it out man!

King Tubby At The Controls 1975 - 1976

A Noise Place - The Aggrovators 1975 (Quiet Place - Horace Andy)
A Ruffer Version - The Aggrovators 1976 (Don't Trouble Trouble - Johnny Clarke)

We started dub with King Tubbys but the man who really pushed version was U Roy and Ruddys from Spanish Town... taking the voice from the rhythm. Tubbys and me had met upstairs at Duke Reid's one day when the version thing came in... it was a mistake made up at Duke Reid's studio. Tubbys and myself was there talking and Ruddys was cutting a dub and Smithy forgot to put in the voice through we were talking and he was going to stop it. Ruddys said *"No. Make it run... let it stay"* and so they cut the pure rhythm. I used to go over and listen to Ruddys and Stereo in Spanish Town. That Saturday night a dance was in progress and they played the vocal to the tune then he said *"Me a go play part two"*. They never called it version and then he played the rhythm track. The song was a catchy song and everybody started to sing. The people just caught the song and sang it over the rhythm. They must have played it about five or ten times and it brought down the house or... as we say in Jamaica... it mashed up the place!

On the Monday I met Tubbys at his studio and I said *"Tubbys... you know the mistake we made upstairs at Duke's studio? It's a serious joke, you know, because the people them love it"*. So I said to Tubbs *"It's a serious thing. It mash up Spanish Town. The people went wild. So we'll have to start to do some of that. You have to start to do that now"*. 'Cause when the man put on the part two everyone start singing this song... it played about twenty times so I said *"you try it Tubbs!"*

In those days I never used to put the version on the record so you'd have to go to Tubbys sound to hear the dub play... it took off and then the people started wanting it on their records. So after that Tubbs started to come like an artist.

Deejays 1970 to 1976

Wake Up The Nation - U Roy & Jeff Barnes 1970

I recorded U Roy before Duke Reid, you know, with a song named 'King Of The Road' … *"here comes the man Lennox Brown with the big horn... The King Of The Road"*. And a song named 'Orgarang'… I just made U Roy introduce 'Bangarang' with Lennox Brown and then another tune with Lester Sterling 'Reggae In The Wind'. When he did it U Roy started in the middle and I got Jeff Barnes from the radio station to come down and talk *"The heights by great men reached and kept were not attained by sudden flight... this brother's been in the musical fight"* till U Roy came in and then you hear the brother with *"Let love shine bright along the way..."* Jeff Barnes made a lot of records too but those were U Roy's first set of tunes.

Cassius Clay - Dennis AlCapone 1973

The tune that really bring Dennis AlCapone up here was 'Cassius Clay' (sings) *"Wah wah gee wah wah..."* Earl 'Wire' Lindo arranged that rhythm too. It's a take off of the 'Drum Song'[1] rhythm but that is his version. Right? And Dennis liked his arrangement with the musicians and everything so Dennis did 'Cassius Clay'… he changed his name to Muhammad Ali[2]… and that tune did bring Dennis AlCapone up here in England (sings) *"Wah wah gee wah wah..."* I'll tell you where that phrase comes from now. Gilbert Roland's words that you know! So we just put it in the tune. Gilbert Roland[3] used to use them words regular… Gilbert Roland and the Mexican people. It's a slang they used so it must have some Spanish meaning. So anyway I just liked the phrase and Dennis said *"Wah wah gee wah wah..."* and it worked.

---

[1] 'Drum Song' – Soul Vendors – Coxsone (Jamaica & CS 7032 UK) 7" 1967
[2] Cassius Clay: the greatest heavyweight boxer of all time, three times Heavyweight World Champion, changed his name to Muhammad Ali (Praiseworthy One) in 1964
[3] Gilbert Roland: Mexican American film actor. Born 11th December 1905. Died 15th May 1994

Straight To Derrick Morgan's Head - I Roy 1975

I started to do a lot of recording with I Roy too and I Roy became like one of the most famous deejays. They used to say him is the most intelligent deejay. The man used to have some great lyrics! I Roy was at Tubby's studio one evening and he left and went away and Prince Jazzbo came in from round the corner with a friend of mine from Canada called George. He used to come and cut specials so the artists got some money too and I used to give him the rhythms. So Jazzbo came and he couldn't do the tune and I Roy came back and said *"Jazzbo man if you was a jukebox I wouldn't put a dime into your slot"* and I said *"Tubbs take this!"* so I put out the tune and Jazzbo said *"Boy... Mr Lee? What kind of joke is that?"* but I said the only thing you can do now is make back a song... I Roy came back with *"Thank you Dirty Harry! We a go a studio right now and make a tune off of it that go clap to their face... Bunny Lee and his brother in law Derrick Morgan"*. It generated some life in a the music business! All of those things happened up at Tubby's...

Strickly Rockers - Jah Stitch 1976

Yes... it came out on a Prophets label! Yabby You used to put out my things! He did an LP with only one Yabby You tune 'pon it... *"Yabby, yabby you..."* all the others were pure Bunny Lee rhythms[1]. So... you know! It was my cut of (sings) *"Just say who..."* Horace Andy [2]... right? Jah Stitch liked it and he used to play a sound named Black Harmony so... one cut! I said *"Jah Stitch you have to record now... you've been around the business too long with Tippertone and all them... (sings) ...Black Harmony killer... then you rock them so"* but he never get shot yet. I brought it up here and gave it to Shaka[3] 'pon a dub and everybody liked it. But after him get shot everybody sad 'cause (sings) *"Black Harmony killer..."* and everybody loved it and said this deejay have potential. It came out on the street and Shelly dropped an LP with him 'No Dread Can't Dead'[4].

---

[1] King Tubby's Prophecies Of Dub – Prestige (Jamaica) LP 1976. There was another Vivian 'Yabby You' Jackson dub LP entitled 'King Tubby's Prophesy Of Dub' - Prophets (UK) LP also from 1976 that actually showcased Yabby You's Prophets rhythms mixed by King Tubby. Vivian 'Yabby You' Jackson Born 14th August 1946. Died 12th January 2010. Self styled 'Jesus Dread' and creator of some of the deepest, most spiritual music ever released

[2] originally a Studio One recording 'Just Say Who' – Horace Andy – Money Disc (Jamaica) 7" 1972

[3] Shaka: Jah Shaka Legendary London based sound system

[4] 'No Dread Can't Dead' – Jah Stitch – Third World TWS 401 (UK) LP 1976

We did all of them LP[1]… because remember Dr Alimantado come 'pon a Shelly album cover first[2]? That time Shelly just catch any dread and put them 'pon an album cover you know… any dread… 'cause the dread business did a go. They start sell dreadlocks wig! You could buy a Rasta tam with some dread hang down round it and you're a Rastaman! You don't remember that?

---

[1] Dread Locks In Jamaica – Various – Live & Love LALP 05 (UK) LP 1976
Straight To Babylon's Chest – Various – Live & Love LALP 06 (UK) 1976
Strictly Rockers In A Dread Land – Various – Live & Love LP 07 (UK) 1976
[2] Straight To Babylon's Chest – Various – Live & Love LALP 06 (UK) 1976 featured a drawing of Winston 'Dr Alimantado' Thompson on the cover

Bunny Lee Now

Sources

Jah Floyd & Noel Hawks: Bunny 'Striker' Lee Interview Part One
London UK 17th August 2006
Jah Floyd & Noel Hawks: Bunny 'Striker' Lee Interview Part Two
London UK 6th December 2006
Noel Hawks: Bunny 'Striker' Lee Interview Part Three
London UK 23rd October 2007
Noel Hawks: Bunny 'Striker' Lee Interview Part Four
London UK 17th September 2008
Jah Floyd & Noel Hawks: Bunny 'Striker' Lee Interview Part Five
London UK 21st October 2009
Jah Floyd & Noel Hawks: Bunny 'Striker' Lee Interview Part Six
London UK 3rd October 2010
Jah Floyd & Noel Hawks: Bunny 'Striker' Lee Interview Part Seven
London UK 24th October 2011
Jah Floyd & Noel Hawks: Bunny 'Striker' Lee Interview Part Eight
London UK 1st March 2012

Noel Hawks: Interview with Bunny 'Striker' Lee
London UK/Kingston Jamaica 2nd March 2010
Noel Hawks: Interview with Bunny 'Striker' Lee
London UK 9th November 2010
Noel Hawks: Interview with Bunny 'Striker' Lee
London UK 16th November 2010
Noel Hawks: Interview with Bunny 'Striker' Lee
London UK/Kingston Jamaica 9th March 2011

Noel Hawks: Interviews with Derrick Harriott
London UK 22nd May 1998 & London UK/Kingston Jamaica 20th June 1998
Noel Hawks: Interviews with Winston Riley
London UK 16th June 1997 & 6th April 1999
Noel Hawks: Interview with Derrick Morgan
London UK/Kingston Jamaica 17th July 2003
Noel Hawks: Interview with Lowell 'Sly' Dunbar
London UK 12th March 2004
Noel Hawks: Interview with Tommy Cowan
London UK/Kingston Jamaica 3rd August 2006
Noel Hawks: Interview with Paul Khouri
London UK/Kingston Jamaica 4th June 2009
Noel Hawks: Interview with Oswald 'Ossie' Hibbert
London UK/New York USA 11th January 2010

Steve Barker: Interview with Clive Chin
Beijing China Friday 6th November 2009
Courtesy of Steve Barker On The Wire BBC Radio Lancashire
Paul Coote: Interview with King Jammy Kingston Jamaica 9th August 1996
Courtesy of Paul Coote
Paul Coote, Dave Hendley & Chris Lane: Interview with Bunny 'Striker' Lee
London UK 3rd September 2000
Courtesy of Paul Coote, Dave Hendley & Chris Lane
Laurence Cane-Honeysett: Interview with Graeme Goodall
London UK/Atlanta USA January 2000
Courtesy of Laurence Cane-Honeysett
Richie 'Reggae Richie' Hanlon: Interview with Bunny 'Striker' Lee
near 90 fm Dublin Eire November 2010
Courtesy of Richie Hanlon
David Rodigan: Interview with Roy 'I Roy' Reid
Capital Radio London UK January 1981
Courtesy of David Rodigan
David Rodigan: Interview with Bunny 'Striker' Lee
BFBS Radio London UK March 1993
Courtesy of David Rodigan
David Rodigan: Interview with Bunny 'Striker' Lee
Kiss FM London UK October 2010
Courtesy of David Rodigan
Adrian Sherwood: Interviews with Prince Jazzbo
London UK/Spanish Town Jamaica June 2000
Courtesy of Pressure Sounds

The Holy Bible Authorised King James Version

Steve Barrow & Peter Dalton: Reggae The Rough Guide
Rough Guides Ltd 1997
Rob Bowman: Soulsville U.S.A. The Story of Stax Records
Books With Attitude 1997
Vivien Morris Brown: The Jamaica Hand Book Of Proverbs
Island Heart Publishers 1993
FG Cassidy & RB Le Page: Dictionary Of Jamaican English Second Edition
University Of The West Indies Press 2002
Alexander Cruden: Cruden's Complete Concordance To The Bible
Lutterworth Press 1990
Roger Dalke: UK Label Discographies (Volumes One to Ten)
Top Sounds International Publications 1982 to 1988

Roger Dalke: Record Selector
(Volumes Five, Fifteen, Sixteen, Seventeen & Eighteen) Top Sounds
International/Tropical Sounds Information Publications 1995 to 2000
Steven Davis & Peter Simon: Reggae International Thames & Hudson Ltd 1983
Michael de Koningh & Laurence Cane-Honeysett: Young, Gifted And Black
The Story Of Trojan Records Sanctuary Publishing Limited 2003
Michael de Koningh & Marc Griffiths: Tighten Up!
The History Of Reggae In The UK Sanctuary Publishing Limited 2003
Christopher Frayling: Spaghetti Westerns
Cowboys And Europeans From Karl May To Sergio Leone IBTauris 2006
Carl Gayle: Are You Ready For Rude And Rough Reggae? Rock File 2
(Edited by Charlie Gillett) Granada Publishing Limited 1974
Laurie Gunst: Born Fi' Dead A Journey Through The Jamaican Posse Underworld
Payback Press 1995
David Katz: People Funny Boy The Genius Of Lee 'Scratch' Perry
Payback Press 2000
David Katz: Nearlin 'Lyn' Taitt Obituary *The Guardian* 11th February 2010
Chris Lane: Bunny Lee The Agro Man
The Reggae Scene *Blues & Soul* 109 11th May 1973
Ian McCann & Harry Hawke: Bob Marley The Complete Guide To His Music
Omnibus Press 2004
Everal McKenzie (Editor): Jamaica Proverbs Blue Mountain Media 2002
Big Al Pavlow: The R&B Book A Disc History Of Rhythm & Blues
Music House Publishing 1983
David Roberts (Managing Editor): British Hit Singles & Albums
Guinness World Records Limited 2005
Robert Schoenfeld: Interview with Lyn Taitt
Dub Catcher Vol. One Issue Four June 1992
Michael Turner & Robert Schoenfeld: Roots Knotty Roots
Nighthawk Records 2001

Steve Barrow: Liner notes Bunny Lee Jumping With Mr Lee 1967 to 1968
(The Producer Series) Trojan TRLS 270 1989
Chris Lane: Liner notes The Big Gundown
(Reggae Inspired By Spaghetti Westerns) Trojan TJCCD062 2004
Chris Lane & Harry Hawking: A Brief History Of Dub Evolution Of Dub
(Parts One to Four) Greensleeves GREW 2007, 2018, 2027 & 2028 2009

Roots Archives: www.roots-archives.com

Acknowledgements

Bunny 'Striker' Lee

With thanks to Annette Wong Lee, Don Lee, Trevor Lee, Dave Lee, Errol Lee, Kirk Lee, Little Striker Lee, Mark Lee, Ann Marie Lee, Bonnie Lee and Tonian Lee. To all the artists, musicians, producers and engineers too numerous to mention here and to Ed Barnes, Jeff Barnes and Winston Williams at RJR, Ken Williams at WLIB, Gil Bailey in New York, David Rodigan MBE at Kiss FM, Steve Barnard & Tony Williams at Radio London, Steve Barrow, David Katz, John Masouri, Patrick 'Stitchie' Feurtado and Ossie Thomas for their support. Thank you all.

Noel Hawks

With grateful thanks, sincere gratitude and love to Anna, Maria and Manny for their endless patience and unfailing support. To Bunny 'Striker' Lee, Jah Floyd and Steve Barrow, Paul Coote, Dave Hendley, Ray Hurford, Naoki Ienaga, Chris Lane, Ian McCann, David Rodigan MBE and Tony Rounce for their patience and generosity in sharing their insight and knowledge.Thank you all.

Jah Floyd

I would like to thank my family, Mum, Joe and Faith. Bunny 'Striker' Lee, Annette Wong Lee and the children for allowing me to be a part of this. Niney The Observer, King Jammy, Ossie Thomas, Tapper Zukie, Diggory Kenrick for all his help with the project, Noel Hawks and all at RAD Print Ltd especially Gary Hall without whom!

About The Authors

Noel Hawks

Noel 'Harry Hawke' Hawks is the author of 'Songs Of Freedom: Complete Lyrics of Bob Marley', co-author, with Ian McCann, of the 2004 edition of 'The Complete Guide To The Music Of Bob Marley', helped to compile 'The Guinness Who's Who Of Reggae' and is currently working on 'Jamaican Recordings: A History Of Jamaica's Recording Studios'. Noel has written on reggae for Billboard, Music Week, Record Collector, Vox and many other magazines and has compiled and written sleeve notes for over 150 reggae releases for Blood & Fire, Fashion, Greensleeves, Jamaican Recordings, Pressure Sounds, Soul Jazz, Trojan and Universal.

Jah Floyd

Over the last decade Jah Floyd has worked closely with Bunny 'Striker' Lee on re-releasing his vast musical catalogue and has compiled and released over 75 reggae albums for Jamaican Recordings and Kingston Sounds.

Designed and Printed by Gary Hall at RAD Printing Ltd

JAMAICAN
RECORDINGS

www.jamaicanrecordings.com

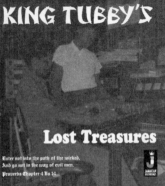

KING TUBBY'S

Lost Treasures

Enter not into the path of the wicked,
And go not in the way of evil men.
Proverbs Chapter 4 No 14.

DJ

JAMAICA INNA FINE DUB STYLE

LEE PERRY

Do not weep: behold, the lion of
the tribe of Juda, the root of
David, has overcome to open the
scroll and its seven seals.
Apocalypse Chapter 5 No 5

...ING WITH THE UPS

RARE DUBS 1971-1974

harry j

DUBBING AT HARRY J'S 1972-1975

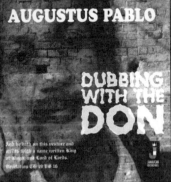

AUGUSTUS PABLO

DUBBING WITH THE DON

And he hath on this vesture and
on his thigh a name written King
of kings and Lord of Lords.
Revelation Ch 19 V 16

Listen up!

WHY FIGHT THE DUB
CONVERSATION DUB
A BETTER VERSION
GENERAL DUB
THE JEHOVAH VERSION
CARE FREE DUB
A WICKED DUB
A TRUTHFUL DUB
ROCKING DUB
STEP INNA DUB STYLE

DUB CLASSI...

THE AGGROVATORS

DUBBING IT STUDIO 1 STYLE

And there was given me a reed like to
a rod, and I was told:
"Rise and measure the temple of God"
Apocalypse Ch 11 No 1

J

JAMAICAN RECORDINGS

THE REVOLUTIONAF...

CHANNEL 1 RECORDING STUDIO

AT CHANNEL 1

DUB PLATE SP...

Put Now Brethen if I come to
you speaking in Tongues what
shall profit you.
Corinthians Chapter 14 No 6

SHALOM DUB

KING TUBBY AND THE AGGROVATORS

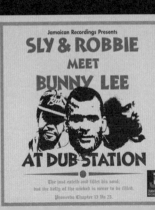

Jamaican Recordings Presents

SLY & ROBBIE
MEET
BUNNY LEE

AT DUB STATION

The just eateth and fillet his soul;
but the belly of the wicked is never to be filled.
Proverbs Chapter 13 No 25.

LEE PERRY PRODUCTIONS

DUB TREASU... FROM THE BLACK...

RARE DUBS 1976-1...

ORACE ANDY'S DUB BOX
RE DUBS 1973-1976

SOUND SYSTEM ROCKERS
KINGSTON TOWN 1969-1975

JAMAICAN RECORDINGS
ORIGINAL JAMAICAN 1970'S DUB
DUB SAMPLER
VOL. 1
100% DUB
NET 13 HEAVY TRACK
PRODUCT OF JAMAIC

SSON ALLSTARS
WITH NG TUBBS
1970

TAPPER ZUKIE
RAGGY JOEY BOY

Listen up!

GORDON WISE U ROY
TRYING TO WRECK BIG JOE
BASH IT UP DR ALIMANTADO
GAL INXY I ROY & PRINCE JAZZBO
BATLIGHT SAVING TIME DILLINGER
JAH IS I GUIDING STAR TAPPER ZUKIE
GASGORS CLAY DENNIS ALCAPONE
STRAIGHT TO PRINCE JAZZBO HEAD
GRUPPLE AND DUAL PRINCE FAR I
WATCH WHAT IS GOING ON U BROWN

DJ STYLE

LINVAL THOMPSON

DUB STORY

KINGSTON
SOUNDS

Niney the Observer

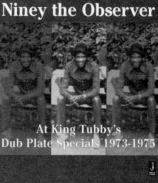

At King Tubby's
Dub Plate Specials 1973-1975

ROOTS
USIC

oston Sounds Sampler

BARRY BROWN'S

STEPPIN UP DUB WISE

SOUNDS
CHANNEL 1
RECORDING STUDIO
33⅓ Rpm
1977-1979
KING JAMMY'S
AT CHANNEL 1
1977-1979

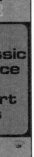

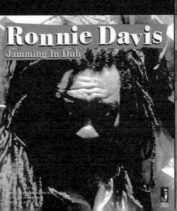

King Jammy's

DUB EXPLOSION

KINGSTON SOUNDS
PRESENTS

U ROY

I AM THE ORIGINATOR

Jamaican Recordings Presents

THE PROFESSIONALS MEET The Aggrovators at JOE GIBBS

BARRY BROWN

LET'S GO TO THE BLUES

DYNAMIC

DUBBING AT DYNAMIC SOUNDS

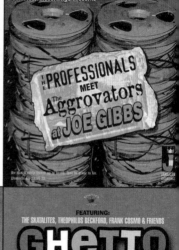

FEATURING:
THE SKATALITES, THEOPHILUS BECKFORD, FRANK COSMO & FRIENDS

GHETTO Ska

FROM THE VAULTS OF WIRL & FEDERAL STUDIOS

DON'T HAVE A TICKET, DON'T WORRY • COME ON MY PEOPLE • MR DOWNPRESSER
FLIP FLOP & FLY • GOODGEFUL PEOPLE • BOILER MAN • HIT YOU LET YOU FEEL IT

DJ
MAICA INNA FINE DUB STYLE

KINGSTON SOUNDS

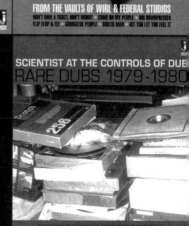

SCIENTIST AT THE CONTROLS OF DUB
RARE DUBS 1979-1980

ROCKSTEADY

HITS THE TOWN

DUB KINGS
KING JAMMY AT KING TUBBY'S

Listen up!

ROOTS NATTY CONGO JOHNNY CLARKE
TRYING YOUTHMAN BARRY BROWN
BAD MINDED PEOPLE LEROY SMART
SKYLARKING HORACE ANDY
TWELVE TRIBES OF ISRAEL LINVAL THOMPSON
BETTER MUST COME DELROY WILSON
MR MONEY MAN BARRY BROWN
POLITRICKS CORNELL CAMPBELL
MONEY MONEY HORACE ANDY
LONG DREADLOCKS LINVAL THOMPSON

ROOTS Reggae

DJ DUBOUTS
Dubbing with the DJ's
Volume 1

DENNIS ALCAPONE
YEAH
YEAH
YEAH
MASH UP THE DANCE

Randy
VINTAGE DUB SELECT
Dubbing at Randy's 1969-1

CORNELL CAMPBELL
The Gorgon Dubwise

TAPPA ZUKIE
★ DUB EM ZUKIE ★
RARE DUBS 1976-1979

KINGSTON SOUNDS
RETURN TO ORANGE STREET
ORANGE STREET
14 ROOTS ROCK REGGAE CLASSICS

KING TUBBY
DUB MIX UP
RARE DUBS 1976-1979

J
JAMAICAN
RECORDINGS

Birth of
Dancehal
BLACK SOLIDARITY 1976

Listen
up!

LASER BEAM DON CARLOS
LOVE TRAP CORNELL CAMPBELL
WICKED THEM A SAY LINVAL THOMPSON
TRIBAL WAR RONNIE DAVIS
MRS LANDLORD TRISTON PALMER
BAD BOY POSSEE ROBERT FRENCH
KING OF THE ARENA JOHNNY CLARKE
GOT TO TELL THE PEOPLE
MR BABYLON ROBERT FRAZER
SATISFACTION JOHNNY CLARKE

Dancehall
ORIGINALS

JAMAICAN RECORDINGS
ORIGINAL 1970'S DUB
JAMAICAN
DUB SAMPLER
100% DUB   VOL. 2   NET 13 HEAVY TRACKS
PRODUCT OF JAMAICA

JA
STITC

DRE
INN
JAN

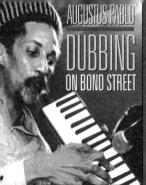
AUGUSTUS PABLO
DUBBING
ON BOND STREET

101 ORANGE STREET
ska meets the rocksteady train

JACKIE MITTOO
RIDES ON

The Congos
FEAST

CORNELL CAMPBELL
MY DESTINATION

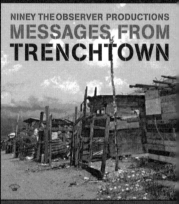
NINEY THE OBSERVER PRODUCTIONS
MESSAGES FROM TRENCHTOWN

PRINCE alla
SØNGS FRØM THE RØYAL THRØNE RØØM

KINGSTON
SOUNDS

DON CARLOS
INNA DUB STYLE
★ Rare Dubs 1979-1980 ★

Skatalites
PLAY
ska

STEREO

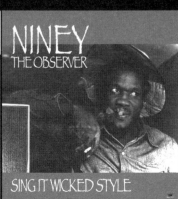
NINEY
THE OBSERVER
SING IT WICKED STYLE

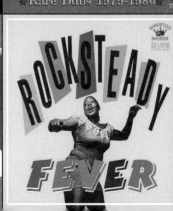
ROCKSTEADY
FEVER

NINEY THE OBSERVER PRODUCTIONS

CHANNEL 1

RECORDING STUDIO

CHANNEL ONE PRESENTS
100 TONS OF DUB

HORACE ANDY
Say Who

JOHNNY CLARKE · DREAD

stereo
The Congos

DUB FEAST

LEROY SMART
J
MR. SMART IN DUB

KINGSTON
SOUNDS

HEAVY STERE
INNA KINGSTON TOU

SOUND SYSTEM ROCKE

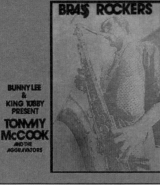

BRA$S ROCKERS

BUNNY LEE &
KING TUBBY
PRESENT
TOMMY McCOOK
AND THE AGGRAVATORS

J
JAMAICAN
RECORDINGS

Pat Kelly

Jam
JS

THE VICEROYS
GHETTO VIBES

KINGSTON
SOUNDS

TAPPA ZUKIE ← → PRODUCTIONS

JAMAICAN J

Horns Up!

DUBBING WITH
HORNS

**Liste
up!**

GORDON MISE - U ROY
TRYING TO WRECK BIG JOE
NASH IT UP DR ALIMANTADO
DAILIGHT SAVING TIME DILLINGER
SAL BOY I ROY & PRINCE JAZZBO
JAH IS I BORDING STAR TAPPER ZUKIE
CASSIUS CLAY DENNIS ALCAPONE
STRAIGHT TO PRINCE JAZZBO HEAD
SHUFFLE AND DEAL PRINCE FAR I
WATCH WHAT IS GOING ON U BROWN

D.
STY